A
Christian Attitude
Toward
Attitudes

Though this book is designed for group study,
it is also intended for personal enjoyment and
spiritual growth. A leader's guide is available
from your local bookstore or your publisher.

Beacon Hill Press of Kansas City
Kansas City, Missouri

Editor
Everett Leadingham

Editorial Assistant
Carolyn Clements

Editorial Committee
Randy Cloud
Everett Leadingham
Thomas Mayse
Carl Pierce
Gene Van Note

Bible Credits

Unless otherwise indicated, all Scripture quotations are taken from the *Holy Bible, New International Version*® (NIV®). Copyright © 1973, 1978, 1984 by International Bible Society. Used by permission of Zondervan Publishing House. All rights reserved.

Quotations from the following copyrighted versions are used by permission:

The *New American Standard Bible* (NASB), © 1960, 1962, 1963, 1968, 1971, 1972, 1973, 1975, 1977 by The Lockman Foundation.

The *New King James Version* (NKJV), copyright © 1979, 1980, 1982, Thomas Nelson, Inc., Publishers.

The Living Bible (TLB), © 1971. Tyndale House Publishers, Inc., Wheaton, IL 60189. All rights reserved.

King James Version (KJV).

10   9   8   7   6   5   4   3

Contents

Your attitude should be the same as that of Christ Jesus: Who, being in very nature God, did not consider equality with God something to be grasped, but made himself nothing, taking the very nature of a servant, being made in human likeness. And being found in appearance as a man, he humbled himself and became obedient to death—even death on a cross! Therefore God exalted him to the highest place and gave him the name that is above every name.

PHIL. 2:5-9

*Keep your face to the sunshine and
you cannot see the shadow.*

HELEN KELLER

*Do not conform any longer to the pattern
of this world, but be transformed by the
renewing of your mind. Then you will be able to
test and approve what God's will is—
his good, pleasing and perfect will.*

ROM. 12:2

BACKGROUND SCRIPTURE
Gen. 50:20; Matt. 5:3-12; Rom. 12:2; 2 Cor. 5:17;
Eph. 4:22-24; Phil. 2:5-11; James 1:2

What Is an Attitude?

by DAVID HOLDREN

THEY CAN SNEAK UP on us like a virus and make us sick. Or, they can do wonders to improve our outlook on life. They can determine the kind of friends we have and, sometimes, how many. They routinely make or break marriages. They shape careers and determine the nature of our influence. They are often contagious. I am convinced that they are one of the most powerful elements of human influence. We are talking about attitudes. Discovering them, dealing with them, and developing them is the theme of these studies. Let's do a little exploring.

What in the World Is an Attitude?

They are more than emotions, yet they affect us emotionally. Attitudes are more enduring than feelings and have longer-lasting impact. They are more than a thought, yet they are fundamentally mental. Their foundation is belief-based. Attitudes are not actions, but they are very influential in shaping our actions and reactions.

Ever noticed how frequently we use the term "attitude"? I keep hearing, "Wow, does she ever have an *attitude!*" That means her negative attitude shows. I recently saw a commer-

---

David Holdren is senior pastor of Cypress Wesleyan Church in Galloway, Ohio.

cial for an automobile with an "attitude." The car was described as "sassy and aggressive."

Tattoos reflect attitudes. "Born to Lose" has been a popular one for some folks. When asked about such a choice, one Chinese tattoo artist said, "Before tattoo on body, tattoo on mind."

Attitudes are like lenses through which we view life. They help shape our actions and our reactions. They are beliefs, assumptions, even prejudices—loaded with emotion.

What is an attitude? It is an emotionally charged belief that regularly affects behavior. It may be the only word in our language that gathers all three primary dimensions of human functioning—beliefs, emotions, and behaviors—and links them.

I would say there are *mega*-attitudes and *mini*-attitudes. Mega-attitudes affect our perspective on daily life. Examples of mega-attitudes are: "I wish I'd never been born," or "People are always out to get me." Or, on a more positive note, "God is never far away, and His hand is on my life." These mega-attitudes tend to be core beliefs that shape overall demeanor and behavior. Although they are replaceable, mega-attitudes tend to be deep-rooted and broad-ranging in their impact.

Mini-attitudes are more focused and temporary, and they are more easily changed. A mini-attitude may be about a specific person, job, or situation. It is not as fleeting as a mood, but it is much more focused in its activity.

What about the Bible and attitudes? Genesis introduces us to a man named Joseph. He was the son of the great patriarch Jacob and had many brothers and one sister. Joseph was a dreamer. He finally told one too many of his self-exalting dreams to his brothers, and they conspired to kill him. The eldest brother intervened and convinced them to put him in a cistern temporarily. The rest of the brothers then sold him as a slave to a group of traveling merchants, who later sold Joseph into slavery in the foreign land of Egypt.

Years passed, and Joseph did remarkably well in spite of the cruel treatment dished out by his family. He became an outstanding leader in the foreign nation and was endowed with vast authority and power.

In yet later years he had the occasion to encounter his brothers when they were totally at his mercy. It seemed that revenge was about to have its sweet opportunity. What would Joseph do to his brothers? What he said revealed his attitude: "You intended to harm me, but God intended it for good to accomplish what is now being done, the saving of many lives" (Gen. 50:20).

What made the difference between mercy and murder in this situation? Attitude. What caused such a gracious and forgiving attitude to develop? Certainly it was not the result of blame, resentment, and self-pity. Joseph's attitude was built on a core belief that a God existed who could redeem bad situations and bring about good results. That belief and God's Spirit enabled Joseph to experience deliverance and avoid bitterness and hatred. He reacted to the situation with great joy, grace, and wisdom.

Where Do We Get Our Attitudes?

Our temperament inclines us to develop and express certain attitudes. Some of us are born with an inclination to be positive and have an upbeat attitude about life in general. Others enter the world more inclined to be pessimistic. Our makeup from birth provides for us some of the raw material for attitude development.

Family and culture shape our attitudes. Children tend to adopt the various perspectives that are held by parents and other early mentors. Those we are around most help form our youthful views and responses.

Life experiences shape our attitudes. A series of negative encounters with men, for example, may incline a woman to form strong negative attitudes about men in general. Or she may acquire negative beliefs about herself that influence her responses to men in particular and life overall.

Often, key individuals influence our attitudes through instruction or example. Such impact may even come through books or other media that communicate attitude messages to us. For Christians, the Bible is a reliable, authoritative, written guide for attitude formation and change.

In Ephesians we are reminded that attitudes are the hinge on which swings any significant change in behavior or lifestyle. Eph. 4:22-24 describes a powerful and practical recipe for change:

1. Bring the old life to a screeching halt.
2. Be made new in the attitude of our minds.
3. Activate the new behavior.

Attitudes are like bridges over which the cargo of life is hauled. These attitude bridges are a vital link between where things have been and where they are going.

Transformation in our lives comes through renewing our points of view that influence so many of our actions and reactions. The apostle Paul indicates that mind renewal is even the key to spiritual transformation for the Christian: "Do not conform any longer to the pattern of this world, but be transformed by the renewing of your mind. Then you will be able to test and approve what God's will is" (Rom. 12:2).

The Can of Paint That Killed Mary

I'll never forget her. Mary was a longtime pillar of a small, conservative congregation in southeastern Ohio. By the time I became acquainted with her, she was a long-term, bitter, church dropout.

I occasionally visited her and learned about her spiritual journey. Finally, I simply asked her why she had abandoned the church and, for the most part, the faith. She told me the story about a bitter disagreement she had with the church trustees over an interior decorating issue. It involved one gallon of paint! Her bitter attitude toward those persons generalized to the church, and even the Lord.

When I officiated at Mary's funeral, I wondered about her early demise and the condition of her soul—maybe all over a can of paint. The real culprit was her attitude.

Attitudes are powerful, for good or ill. They can supply the positive power to overcome incredible odds, or they can prompt negative responses that can destroy any relationship in our lives.

Emotions are also a forceful motivator, but they can change rapidly and are not the best foundations for decisions and actions.

Beliefs are the framework for our actions; but even beliefs do not always lead to action, unless they are emotionally charged.

Attitudes combine beliefs with emotions to bring about the likelihood of action. In a review of the Scriptures, I uncovered the phrase "a spirit of," which seemed to be similar to our use of the term "attitude." For example, "a spirit of despair" (Isa. 61:3) was to be replaced by "a garment of praise" through the Lord's anointed preacher. "A spirit of prostitution" (Hos. 4:12) was leading the priests and people of Israel away from God. "A spirit of grace and supplication" (Zech. 12:10) is what the Lord promised to pour out on Israel. "A spirit of unity" (Rom. 15:5) was Paul's prayer for the Christians at Rome. And Paul reminded Timothy that "God has not given us a spirit of fear, but of power and of love and of a sound mind" (2 Tim. 1:7, NKJV).

In His early teachings, Jesus provides a set of spiritual foundations that we could call the "Be-attitudes" (Matt. 5:3-12). They deal with such core attitudes as humility, empathy, mercy, and spiritual hunger. Jesus reminds us that certain attitudes are the bridges to spiritual blessing and ultimate destinations in and beyond this life.

Attitudes are the launching pads for the most important

actions and reactions in life. Attitudes are not the way the winds are blowing, but the way our sails are set.

We Are Responsible for Our Attitudes

Great news! We can choose our attitudes. Though they may develop subtly, we can identify and change them. However, this is often a process that requires time and outside help.

In 2 Cor. 5:17, Paul gives us a tremendous statement about those who are in Christ being new creations. In what ways are we new? The previous verse indicates that a new "point of view" (attitude) is the key to new life. The message is that Christ helps change us from the inside out.

Take time to read Phil. 2:5-11. In that passage the writer says, "Your attitude should be the same as that of Christ Jesus: Who . . . did not consider equality with God something to be grasped" (vv. 5-6).

One more scripture: "Consider it pure joy, my brothers, whenever you face trials of many kinds" (James 1:2). What a wild and strange statement! Was this a slip of the pen, or was the writer fresh from a spiritual renewal meeting and still feeling invincible? A fair paraphrase of this verse might be, "Look at hard times from a thoroughly positive and faithful frame of reference." The writer seems to state the existence of a belief that embraces the emotions and affects our actions and, especially, our reactions.

Attitudes are life-changing and life-shaping. Attitudes are constantly at work shaping the essence of our responses to life, like a vital organ in our bodies that is constantly doing its task. Yet attitudes are always in the process of being developed themselves.

Attitude Transformation Is a Must

We are responsible for our attitudes. Why? Because we can choose them, and we can change them. How? Here are several ways:

1. Identify core attitudes about God, life, and people, even about past and present situations. Which attitudes are positive and helpful? Which ones incline to negative, counterproductive, or even sinful directions? Use the light of God's Word, and invite the Holy Spirit to search and inform. Identify the most helpful and the most destructive attitudes.

2. Confess and commit them to God. Thank God for the good ones and build on them. Repent of the destructive ones and determine to seek transformation.

3. Begin, with the help of God and a trusted friend, to re-fashion strategic attitudes. This usually takes time because it is a multiple-stage process. Past issues need to be mended, and a new framework of values and viewpoints needs to be carved out. Determine how a given attitude needs to change. Be specific. Be biblical. Seek whatever counsel is needed.

4. Pay attention to the results. After the attitude adjustments, are actions and reactions to the same kind of situations different than before? Feelings and behaviors are the best indicators of truly changed beliefs. Are the three becoming more consistent with one another? If so, a new attitude exists. Enjoy it. Others will too.

Most banks have an outdoor service that has been called an ATM, which stands for "automated teller machine." Let's give those common letters a new meaning. Each time we pull into our local bank and see the ATM, we can think of those letters as meaning "Attitude Transformation is a Must!" It is.

Begin an attitude inventory today. Let it become a lifelong process of personal, spiritual growth. Conversion of our attitudes is an important part of God's continuing work of grace in our lives. Where do we need to begin?

A proud man is seldom a grateful man,
for he never thinks he gets as much
as he deserves.

HENRY WARD BEECHER

The mind of sinful man is death,
but the mind controlled by the Spirit
is life and peace.

ROM. 8:6

BACKGROUND SCRIPTURE
Pss. 32:1-2; 56:9; John 14:27;
Rom. 5:3-6; 8:28, 31; 12:1; 2 Cor. 4:7-9;
Phil. 2:5-8; 4:7; Col. 1:10-14; 3:3-4; Heb. 6:19-20

A Christian Perspective on Attitude

by N. KEITH HINTON

A LIFELONG FRIEND, and my pastor for over 14 years, Rev. G. R. Bateman, was fond of saying, "It doesn't matter what happens as much as it matters what my attitude is *toward* what happens."

As a teenage parishioner and later as his pastor, I was able to observe closely his Christian attitude in many different circumstances of life. I watched him in the good times and the bad, in times of triumph and defeat, in times of joy and in deep sorrow. After over 32 years of observation I'm happy to say his attitude has never disappointed me. He has always maintained a positive Christian attitude.

Such consistency in attitudes is based on more than "positive thinking" or "positive mental attitude." It arises from a source other than "the power within us" expounded by the New Age movement. Christian attitudes are deeply rooted in the truth of God's Word and the realization of God's power at work in our lives.

N. Keith Hinton is senior pastor of Trinity Wesleyan Church in Jackson, Michigan. He has been married for 25 years and is the father of two sons and one daughter.

Christ, Our Example

The beginning and the end of all proper Christian attitudes is Jesus. The excellent Scottish preacher of holiness, Dr. John S. Logan, used to say with conviction, "Holiness is Christlikeness." The first time I heard him quote that phrase I was struck by its profound simplicity. Surely he was right. The essence of a holy lifestyle, including attitudes, is our imitation of Christ.

Speaking of humility, the apostle Paul told the Philippian church their "attitude should be the same as that of Christ Jesus" (2:5). That is not only true of humility but also true of every attitude we may exhibit. For an outlook to be truly Christian, it must truly reflect Christ.

Not only is Jesus our Example, but also His Holy Spirit within us is our Source. It has been suggested that genuine Christian attitudes spring up primarily from three Christian attributes. Each of these graces are rooted in the person and ministry of Jesus Christ. They are *joy, peace,* and *hope*—each representing a certain perspective on life that positively affects our daily attitudes.

The Joy That Jesus Brings

Probably no greater source of joy can be found than the wonderful reality of sins forgiven. "What happiness for those whose guilt has been forgiven! What joys when sins are covered over! What relief for those who have confessed their sins and God has cleared their record" (Ps. 32:1-2, TLB).

Through the years I have witnessed the freedom, excitement, and emotional responses of those who experience the joy of forgiveness. A man in one of my congregations would often be overcome with emotion while sitting in a service. He said he would begin to remember the sinful life he had led and the forgiveness he had received through Christ. He would try to suppress it. When he could contain it no longer, he would leap to his feet with tears of joy coursing down his cheeks and emotionally blurt out, "I'm having such a good time serving the Lord!"

Another pastor reported that once, as he raised a convert from the baptismal water, the new Christian was clapping his hands and shouting, "Hot dog, hot dog, hot dog!" It seemed to be the only way he knew to express the joy he felt in having his sins forgiven.

Of course, it would be quite unusual for us to live each day on that kind of emotional high. However, the joy behind the emotion is valid throughout our lifetime of walking with God. This is blessedness that comes from knowing of God's favor toward us, experiencing His great love, and discovering His concern about our lives. It is gladness that persists even in discouraging circumstances of life. It is comfort resulting from the assurance that no matter what, "God is for me" (Ps. 56:9). "If God is for us, who can be against us?" (Rom. 8:31).

The joy we have as Christians is not dependent on circumstances. It is easy to be joyful when everything is going well, but quite another story to have this joy in the dark places of our lives. Someone has said, "If joy is not rooted in the soil of suffering, it is shallow." This abiding sense of genuine joy will produce attitudes that our unbelieving friends will not really understand, but which could lead to opportunities for explaining our Source of joy.

Paul reminds us in the first chapter of Colossians that we should "live a life worthy of the Lord" (v. 10). Part of that worthy life is "joyfully giving thanks to the Father" (vv. 11-12) for "the forgiveness of sins" (v. 14). The joy that Jesus brings through forgiveness of our sins is the beginning of joyful attitudes that should be characteristic of Christian living.

The Peace That Jesus Gives

In addition to joy, peace serves as a basis for Christian attitudes. This peace is the result of the abiding presence of the Holy Spirit in our life. For the sanctified believer, peace comes from knowing that we are no longer at odds with the purposes and plans of the Father. It is the peace of full surrender and complete consecration to God. Having presented ourselves as "living sacrifices" (Rom. 12:1), we experience the serenity of fully trusting our Heavenly Father with every detail of our lives.

It was this composure, exhibited in Moravian Christians, that first alerted John Wesley to his need of a personal Savior. On board ship en route to Georgia, Wesley observed their peace of mind in every circumstance. Even in the storms, while he shook with fear and others screamed with terror, the Moravians seemed calm and secure. Later, Wesley commented that the Moravians knew something he did not yet know. They had prepared him to seek personal assurance of salvation.

When Jesus said, "Peace I leave with you" (John 14:27), He said it in conjunction with the "Counselor" role of the Holy Spirit (e.g., v. 26). There is no peace apart from His presence. There is no lasting comfort outside of His counsel. The Holy Spirit guides and directs our lives. He pleads our case as our Advocate with the Father, and He "stands alongside" us in the midst of any trouble. He teaches us the truth as we read God's Word. His abiding presence in us is our assurance that we are the children of God, and He communicates to us the very mind of Christ. This is the peace that Jesus gives. It cannot be duplicated by the world.

Georges Simenon, one of the most-translated authors in the world, has written over 400 novels. Explaining why he wrote so much, he said, "I have only one ambition left, to be completely at peace with myself. I doubt if I shall ever manage it. I do not think it is possible for anyone."[1] Clearly, no matter what our device or plan for accomplishing inner peace, it cannot be found outside the abiding Spirit of Jesus in our lives.

Yet, like joy, this peace is not really complete until it meets face-to-face with the difficulties of living. It isn't just that we have an attitude of calm assurance about us, it is that we can exhibit a sense of peace even in the midst of life's most trying circumstances. The sanctified heart really believes that "in all things God works for the good of those who love him" (Rom. 8:28). Through the tears of deepest sorrow, that soul can still reflect the peace of God through Christ, "which transcends all understanding" (Phil. 4:7).

One artist pictured this peace by painting a powerful waterfall with winds blowing the spray of the water in many directions. On a limb, hanging out over the water, a bird had built its nest and sat peacefully upon her eggs. Here she would be safe from her enemies, though dangling over the perilous falls. What a beautiful illustration of the peace that Jesus gives! It is a peace that will help us demonstrate Christlike attitudes in all of life.

The Hope That Jesus Inspires

Hope is not unique to Christianity. Our world speaks of hope often and believes it to be a driving force for future improvement. We hope for a cure to diseases like AIDS. We hope for a solution to the crime problem. We hope for stability in economic conditions. Such hope is really nothing more than an optimistic view of the future—a belief that the future will be better than today. Some solutions may be found in the years to come, but other answers will never be discovered outside the gospel of Jesus Christ.

Although hope is not unique to Christianity, New Testament hope is far more than the wishful thinking of the world. The hope spoken of in the Gospels is anchored in reality. Dr. Charles W. Carter, noted Wesleyan scholar and author, has stated that hope is a stronger word than faith in the New Testament. Faith speaks of anticipation, while hope conveys apprehension of that which is desired. Hope embraces and "lays hold upon." Hope is anchored in God himself. The letter to the Hebrews says, "We have this hope as an anchor for the soul, firm and secure. It [hope, the anchor] enters the inner sanctuary behind the curtain, where Jesus, who went before us, has entered on our behalf" (6:19-20). In Carter's words, "Hope enters into the veil and lays hold upon" Jesus, our "High Priest forever."[2]

In his letter to the Roman church, Paul gave us reason to rejoice even in our sufferings. He reminded us that "suffering produces perseverance; perseverance, character; and character, hope. And hope does not disappoint us" (5:3-5). This hope is not just a trust for eternal life, though that is involved. It is a belief based in the ultimate triumph of good over evil. It is a faith that speaks of our own personal identification with that ultimate triumph and literally rests all of its expectations on the loving character of God.

The idea may be illustrated as a competition taking place in our lives. God urges us to hope in Him, while the world says we should hope in worldly methods. As we encounter each test, we must decide whether or not to do things God's way or the world's way. Often, the world's way seems more obvious and even logical; but to be victorious, we choose to follow God's direction. In doing that, we take a "chance" (so to speak), because God doesn't always reveal the rightness of His ways immediately. Indeed, we may not know exactly why His way is best until we get to heaven. Therefore, we hope.

Through each tribulation in which we persevere successfully we build more hope. Eventually, our whole life has been lived, depending not on the world's values or recognition but on our hope in God. Yet this is not just ordinary trust, for "hope [in God] does not disappoint us" (Rom. 5:5a). Our hope is based on God's love for us, which He has "poured out . . . into our hearts by the Holy Spirit" (v. 5b). He has demonstrated the practicality of His love in that "when we were still powerless, Christ died for [us]" (v. 6). Though the world may not recognize or understand it, we know God's love is real because it is living within us. Our hope will prove well-founded, because God—who has done so much for us already—will not forsake us in the end. He will ultimately set all records straight.

With this kind of hope living within us, it is easy to see why the Christian's attitudes should be positive and optimistic. Perhaps even more than the joy of sins forgiven or the peace that Jesus gives is the influence of the hope that Christ inspires in all of us. The Christian's upbeat, victorious attitude grows out of the fact that one day our Lord will return to earth in triumph. If our "life is now hidden with Christ in God," then "when Christ, who is [our] life, appears, . . . [we] also will appear with him in glory" (Col. 3:3-4).

Joy, peace, and hope form the basis for Christian attitudes that are different from the attitudes of the world. However, let us be quick to add that even the fully surrendered believer is still human. Our attitudes will still be influenced by our emotional state, our changing circumstances, and other such matters. "But we have this treasure in jars of clay to show that this all-surpassing power is from God and not from us. We are hard pressed on every side, but not crushed; perplexed, but not in despair; persecuted, but not abandoned; struck down, but not destroyed" (2 Cor. 4:7-9).

Christians have a joy that is deeper than emotions, a peace that is greater than circumstances, and hope that is anchored in more than wishful thinking.

---

1. Paul Lee Tan, *Encyclopedia of 7,700 Illustrations: Signs of the Times* (Garland, Tex.: Bible Communications, 1979), 988.

2. Taken from my personal notes of a lecture delivered by Dr. Carter during a graduate class in 1984.

*No man is more unhappy than the one who
is never in adversity; the greatest affliction
of life is never to be afflicted.*
ANONYMOUS

*Who shall separate us from the love of Christ?
Shall trouble or hardship or persecution
or famine or nakedness or danger or sword?*
ROM. 8:35

BACKGROUND SCRIPTURE
Ps. 118:24; Phil. 2:5; 4:11-13

3

Attitudes Under Pressure

by DONALD E. DEMARAY

PERHAPS THE GREATEST discovery of a person's life is this: *I can change my life by altering my attitude.*

If I want to live in a grousing, complaining world, I must decide to have a negative outlook. If, on the other hand, I want to take up residence in a happy, joyful world, I can do that by firm decision making. I can learn to do that habitually and daily.

The ancient writer Horace penned powerful words about a right attitude. He said only a "fool finds fault with a place. The fault is not there but in the mind." More, the fool changes his sky, but not his mind. He runs across the sea, but what he seeks "is here, in every meanest village," if he maintains a balanced and serene temper. The great thinker admonishes: "Prepare what will make you a friend to your own self."[1]

Not what happens to me, but how I react to what happens, determines the way I see life. So the apostle Paul, writing from prison, declared, "I have learned to be content whatever the circumstances" (Phil. 4:11).

We Can Choose to Be Miserable

An older woman came for counsel. "I'm miserable," she

Dr. Donald E. Demaray is professor of preaching at Asbury Theological Seminary in Wilmore, Kentucky.

began. She spelled out a sad scenario. Really, an elongated series of complaints.

She said she wanted help. Gently, but firmly, I told her about the great discovery one can make: *We can change our lives by altering our attitude.* Would you believe she walked away? Her body language announced clearly, "I will not change my negative attitudes. I want to enjoy the luxury of complaining. I like the attention—the ego massaging—I get."

So she didn't want help after all. Evidently, she was not aware of the power of attitude. It's more important than facts. It's more significant than what's happened. Than learning. Money. Circumstances. Mistakes. Successes. Even greater than what anyone thinks about us, says or does to us. It surpasses appearance and one's gifts or skills. Attitude can make or break a corporation, a church, a home.

Here's the clincher: *I have a daily choice.* I can embrace each new morning with a good attitude or a bad one. I cannot change the inevitable, but I can play on the "one string" I have—my attitude. It is true that life is only 10% what happens to me, but 90% how I react to it.

There's a practical way to integrate a positive attitude. Buy a notebook small enough to carry in pocket or purse, and record praises—only praises—in it. Do it daily. Thank God in these written prayers for even small blessings. Like these:

- When the driver ran the red light yesterday, he missed me.
- I have a beautiful garden this year: radishes, lettuce, Alaska peas, two kinds of onions.
- The rain last night made my yard green again.
- I feel close to my friends.

A really helpful way to begin and close a day is to thank God specifically for His many mercies.

I alone am in charge of my attitude. No one else controls the kind of world I see and live in. I can say often, "This is the day the LORD has made; let us rejoice and be glad in it" (Ps. 118:24).

The Pressure of Tragedy

I often hear people say, "But you don't know what happened to me!" But I know what happened to Marshall Shelley. His stories are tragic—the death of his retarded daughter, Mandy, and his infant son, Toby. Toby was short for Tobiah, which means "God is good"; but he lived only two minutes! Marshall got angry at God; yet he and Susan, his wife, faced heartache head-on.

Their seven-year-old daughter, Stacey, heard a voice in the middle of the night that said, "Mandy and Toby are very busy. They are building our house, and they're guarding His throne." Marshall admits he does not know what "guarding His throne" means—does God need His throne guarded?—but he believes his two little ones stay meaningfully occupied in heaven. That revelation brought a whole new attitude to the Shelleys. It gave them an attitude that once more made life worth living, fully and joyfully.[2]

The Pressure of Persecution

Chinese Christians inspire me. They go beyond merely putting up with their circumstances. They engage in aggressive, joyous evangelism. Forty-five years ago China counted 5 million Christians. Today's estimates: up to 75 million! That despite the sure fact that many Christians died in the Cultural Revolution of 1966-76.

Today one would think the Cultural Revolution has not really come to an end, because Chinese Christians, like the early Christians in Acts, suffer a lot of persecution. The "true freedom of religion" China's government talks about just doesn't happen consistently. Christians often find themselves arrested for their faith, fined, sent to prison, even tortured. The government cries out against house gatherings, Bible teaching to youth, evangelistic travel, listening to religious radio, distributing Christian publications. They even oppose healing prayers!

Does this stop the Chinese Christians? No! A thousand

times no! They get out of prison and go right back to witnessing. Like first-century Christians, they see people come to Christ. No torture stops them—not hanging upside down, not even beatings with wire. The clear witness from such suffering is that these Christians actually find joy because they love God and their fellow Chinese so much.

What is the source of this remarkable attitude? They have *chosen* to follow the dynamic Spirit of Jesus Christ living inside them rather than give in to the maltreatment.

The Pressure of Depression

A decisive change of attitude can work very well for about 95% of the population. But some people suffer from a paralyzing depression that prevents the deeply desired change of attitude that sees life as good. These people may, in fact, be victims of bad genetics, like some who have high blood pressure because they inherited it. In any case, we can know by a simple blood test if one must go on medication.

If we think our attitudes are the result of chemical imbalance, what can we do?

Go to the doctor. Joe went through life with lots of ups and downs—sometimes happy with his wife and home, sometimes unhappy. He alternated between being terribly angry and being calm, almost carefree.

What Joe required was medication to control the mood swings. He needed to see a doctor. Yet, he refused to come to terms with his problem, despite the agony it caused him and his family. Now, at the end of his life, he lies in a rest home, often depressed, not really wanting to see anyone—not even his wife, children, or grandchildren.

Fear often keeps people from getting the help needed. Sometimes family members can create an atmosphere that puts fears to rest and opens a door to assistance. If we or someone we love needs help, we should find a way to get it.

Realize that most paralyzing depressions have bound-

aries—they come to an end. Bill was very sensitive and perceptive. He saw his faults too well and feared people did not like him. He often felt inhibited and threatened. Authority figures especially bothered him. He went through many years trying to find fulfilling ways to get people to like him. His fears caused him to believe he suffered social skills deficiencies.

With wise support from family members and affirmation by elders in church and school, Bill adjusted normally. In fact, he became an outstanding leader, helping other people find their way through the purgatory he had overcome.

A word of caution might help: Encourage sensitive young people to get outside themselves, to get involved in positive activities. Often, feeling something is amiss, they dig into their inner selves, reading psychology books, spending excessive time thinking—all in the attempt to cure themselves. Some even go on street drugs as a self-help way of finding therapy. Very bright young people often entertain thoughts of suicide because their peers isolate them. They need a clear sense of acceptance wherever they can get it.

A further word of caution: Exercise patience. We have no sure way of knowing how long a particular individual will take to mature. But we can always listen lovingly. We can provide medical help and counseling from Christian professionals. We should keep alert to the Spirit's directions. By contrast, we know impatience, irritation, and forcing therapy will retard healing, even worsen depression at times.

Our goal as Christians is to enable even depressed persons to get to the point of making a basic decision about attitude, a decision that will create possibilities for a hopeful, joyful, and productive life.

Get spiritual help. Mary Jane, a social worker, enjoyed seven years of fulfilling work. She helped people. She loved getting up in the morning, knowing she would spend her day assisting people, often people in desperate straits.

Her life changed when her position was eliminated. She

moved back to her hometown and took the only job she could find. But she was dissatisfied. She felt a divine call to the former type of employment. Because she could not go back to her old position, she slid into depression.

She sought help from a minister who believed in healing. He gave her E. Stanley Jones's book *Abundant Living*. That book bombarded her with a large volley of new insights. Little by little she saw herself in new light, especially in the light of God's love for her.

God's grace kept her searching until counseling, reading, prayer, and journaling created a new self-perception. She saw herself with a future. She tackled her current employment with a sense of divine call. She began to experience job satisfaction. One day she realized she was really free of depression. She was healed!

Alfred's case is unusual. He needs a lot of sunlight. Winter days and dark places threaten to rob him of his normally bright attitude. The disease he has makes sleep a hit-and-miss endeavor and causes severe pain. He must attack the problem actively in several ways:

- Exercising out of doors (like bike riding or hiking)
- Taking medication to control pain and to insure sleep
- Making a firm decision to maintain a good attitude "in spite of"

He does the latter by monitoring his speech (no negative talk), disciplined Bible reading and prayer (heaven's therapy!), and the deliberate exercise of faith. He's winning! Some days hit him pretty hard, but what impresses family and friends most is his winning attitude and his contagious personality. He almost never mentions his disease, and he never complains. He often talks about Scripture, the character development of the group of boys he leads, and the advances of his local church. In short, he embraces an "attitude of gratitude."

The Pressure of Negative News

Brad and Mary take life seriously. They see life as ominous. Never missing the news hour, they know too well the sad events of the world. They persist in talking about problems, even problems they cannot control—the weather, wars overseas, organized crime in Europe. They keep themselves in a stew.

True, they are Christians, but they live in Good Friday more than Easter. They so dislike evil society with its opposition to biblical morality that they always feel depressed.

This negative posture creates a set of disturbing questions for them: How can people pay bills promptly with galloping inflation? Do parents really have a chance to rear good kids today? How does the boss expect one to find time to learn new technology and still get the job done? The questions are so forceful and frequent they block off their creative, imaginative instincts. Brad had a nervous breakdown and had to quit his job for several months. After that, Mary lived an even more disturbed and hectic life.

How can we avoid Brad and Mary's situation? Here are some helpful suggestions:

- Nip negative thinking in the bud. Choose not to do it.
- Take control of what we discuss. Monitor TV viewing, reading, and the company we keep to avoid negative influences.
- Especially, choose a positive thought style. Paul never wrote anything more practical than Phil. 4:11-13:

     I am not saying this because I am in need, for I have learned to be content whatever the circumstances. . . . I know what it is to have plenty. I have learned the secret of being content in any and every situation, whether well fed or hungry, whether living in plenty or in want. I can do everything through him who gives me strength.

How can we all remember: **Stop! Look! Listen!**

- Stop negative thinking.

- Look at the blessings in life.
- Listen to positive voices.

We can decide to look at life today with a positive attitude. We can refuse to let circumstances dictate our mood. We can choose to let our "attitude . . . be the same as that of Christ Jesus" (Phil. 2:5).

---

1. *Epistles*, 11.27.
2. Marshall Shelley, "Two Minutes to Eternity," *Christianity Today* 38 (May 16, 1994): 25 and "The Sightless, Wordless, Helpless Theologian," *Christianity Today* 37 (April 26, 1993): 34.

Earth hath no sorrow that heaven cannot heal.

THOMAS MOORE

Be merciful to me, O LORD, for I am in distress;
my eyes grow weak with sorrow,
my soul and my body with grief.

PS. 31:9

BACKGROUND SCRIPTURE
Ps. 42:3, 5; Prov. 23:7; Matt. 26:38; Rom. 12:2;
2 Cor. 1:8; Eph. 4:23; Phil. 4:8

4

More than the Blues

by LES PARROTT III

MIKE, A SOLDIER I KNOW who returned from the war called Desert Storm, landed in another storm he did not train for—postwar depression. He didn't know why he turned inward and withdrew from his friends and loved ones who had prayed for his safe return. And they didn't understand his strange behavior, either.

Ron is a deep-voiced, sincere, committed pastor in his 50s. He has been troubled by thoughts of death and the seeming futility of his ministry that never really catches fire. For weeks, he hasn't had the energy to open his mail.

Cindy, an elegant woman with a reputation for professional competence, has been obsessed with unaccountable thoughts of not meeting the demands of her fast-paced job. After months of sleeplessness and feelings of worthlessness, she quit—to the consternation of her employers and family. She now sees little hope for her future and often stays in bed sobbing until lunchtime.

John is a missionary who was sent home from a third-world country with instructions to seek professional help for

Les Parrott III is a clinical psychologist, a professor at Seattle Pacific University in Seattle, and an ordained minister in the Church of the Nazarene. This article first appeared with the title "Do Christians Get Depressed?" in the December 1991 issue of *Herald of Holiness*.

his flagging spirit and strange new bouts of irritability and anger toward both his colleagues and the people he was trying to serve. After 25 years of service, he sees life as meaningless and thinks of destroying himself.

Sara, 17, broke up with her boyfriend some weeks ago. Since then, she has lost interest in church and school. She stopped reading her Bible and pays her school assignments little attention. She blames herself for the breakup and doesn't think she will ever again have a boyfriend. At times, she wonders if the world would be better off without her.

Each of these people is experiencing what 5 million other Americans struggle with every year: *depression.*

We are experiencing depression in unprecedented numbers. Recent studies report that depression is 10 times more prevalent today than it was 50 years ago. One of its consequences, suicide, takes as many lives as the AIDS epidemic and is more widespread. Depression now strikes a full decade earlier in life on the average than it did in the previous generation. Sometimes it strikes without warning and in unaccountable ways. Often, depression creeps up silently like a cat. This scourge of the spirit and mind may last a few days, or maybe years if not treated.

When a person becomes a casualty to depression, it doesn't take a mental health professional to know something is wrong. The victim is miserable, and all the people his or her life touches are either miserable, confused, or both.

Is Depression a Sin?

Emotions—especially negative emotions—often trouble spiritually sensitive believers who are trying to cope with adult problems using half-grown emotional skills and immature theology picked up unexamined from their religious environment. While we accept physical pain and disease as normal, we sometimes treat emotional pain as if it were a criminal offense or an evil curse.

I have counseled many Christians who believe erroneously that their depression is a sign of spiritual failure. Some want to call it sin and then wallow in their own guilt. After all, they argue, how can a Christian—especially a sanctified Christian—be depressed?

However, this erroneous understanding of the cause of guilt is not supported in the Scriptures. Job, Moses, and Jonah are examples of God's persons who fought bouts of depression. After a stunning victory on Mount Carmel, Elijah is next seen sitting alone and depressed under a twisted juniper tree in the desert, despairing of his life. Certainly David experienced depression. The Psalms abound with evidences of depression such as this one: "My tears have been my food day and night . . . Why are you downcast, O my soul?" (42:3, 5).

In the New Testament, Matthew reports on the depressing mental pressure Jesus suffered in Gethsemane as He prayed, "My soul is overwhelmed with sorrow to the point of death" (26:38). During a time of depression, it is easy to feel like God has forgotten.

Even Paul, the missionary saint who strode fearlessly into the city synagogues of Asia proclaiming Christ and forging the theology that was to forever guide the Church, had his own problems with depression. "We were under great pressure," he writes in 2 Corinthians, "far beyond our ability to endure, so that we despaired even of life" (1:8).

Biographies of the saints don't square with the mistaken reasoning of modern Christians who blame depression on their spiritual state. Martin Luther, Charles Spurgeon, and John Wesley all suffered at times from depression. Samuel Logan Brengle, the great saint of the Salvation Army whose writings on holiness have helped millions to a deeper Christian faith, was so familiar with depression he referred to it as his "old acquaintance."

Let's make this matter clear. *Depression is not necessarily a sign of spiritual failure.* Often, personal healing only begins after the Christian has accepted this fact. Spiritualizing a problem that is psychological or physiological in nature hinders attempts to get at the root of the problem, just as psychologizing a spiritual problem hinders spiritual healing. Sin is not simply a psychological problem, and depression is not necessarily a sin problem.

Why Good People May Become Depressed

While it is difficult to identify a specific cause of depression, researchers have isolated clusters of probable causes, and most agree that depression is the result of a combination of these causes.

Genetic vulnerability and our biology. Although it is not believed that people actually inherit depression like they inherit the color of their eyes, there is enough research to suggest that people can inherit a predisposition to depression. Studies conducted since the 1930s show depression to be eight times more likely in biological parents than in the adoptive parents of depressed adoptees. Some researchers also believe that, in certain cases, changes in hormone levels contribute to depressed feelings.

While physical causes can be quite complicated (e.g., glandular disorders, brain tumors, etc.), they can also be as simple as medication side effects, improper diet, or lack of sleep. Physical causes of depression, however, only account for a small portion of the people in our depression-prone culture who suffer from this debilitating condition.

Life experience. Not even the most severe of situations has the power in itself to produce depression. Viktor Frankl, describing conditions within the Nazi death camps of World War II, recalled individuals who spent their time encouraging and comforting others. Nevertheless, certain situational factors do seem to increase one's susceptibility to depression. The loss of a significant relationship, a job, or even a dream can increase the risk of depression. So can prolonged exposure to stressful conditions. Randy, an adolescent I have worked with, grew up with parents who set their expectations and standards far beyond his abilities. Failure was inevitable. Depression was the result.

Social rewards. Some experts assert that people become and remain depressed because of the reward they obtain when they appear sad in front of others. The sympathy and concern they receive, in other words, ironically reinforces their depression.

Sharon was a woman with poor social skills and, consequently, had few close friends. Her everyday life was uneventful and empty. In time, she became depressed. She confided to several people at church that she was feeling very down. Suddenly, the church community came alive for her. The pastor called regularly. Friends began telephoning, helping with chores, and even sitting with her through the night. Almost instantaneously, she gained a warm and supportive community.

She began feeling better, and as she did, her friends went back to their previous business. What do you think happened next? Indeed. She became depressed again. Why? Because life, in one sense at least, was more pleasant, more bearable for her when she was depressed. The well-meaning people who comfort a depressed person can potentially be sustaining the symptoms if the attention is only given when the person's behavior is unhealthy.

Learned helplessness. People can also become depressed when they think they have no control. Walter, an employee for a large company, came to believe there was nothing he could do to earn his boss's approval. He attributed this problem to his personal inability to succeed, and he saw it as a situation that would last for years. This pessimistic combination of seeing the circumstance as his own fault and as being long-term is what Martin Seligman, a psychologist at the University of Pennsylvania, calls "learned helplessness." Walter sees his actions as futile, no matter how hard he tries. Depression is inevitable.

Faulty logic. Irrational thinking is at the core of many cases of depression. I have worked with numerous high school and college students who think they are a "total failure" because they didn't say the right thing at the lunch table. Adults do the same thing. We selectively concentrate on a single mistake to convince ourselves we are worthless. When we feel inadequate, or view life as a burden, or see our future as going nowhere, we are likely to trigger a downward spiral of depression that reinforces our negative expectations.

Coping with Depression

Just about everyone gets mildly depressed on occasion. On any given day, 25% of Americans say they're "melancholy." About 40% claim they've had 5 to 10 "blue" days in a year. It seems mild depression is the psychological equivalent of the common cold. It springs from the pain and loss that are inevitable parts of being human. We don't get the jobs we want. We get rejected by people we love. The result of such losses is regular and predictable. We feel sad, pessimistic, and helpless. We become passive and lethargic. Life goes sour.

Depression, however, has a worthwhile function. It triggers a series of responses in the body to deal with the chaos in life. It is a natural and normal response that forces us to withdraw from a troublesome environment to regain perspective and make appropriate adjustments. Much misery is caused by believing that mild depression is always unnecessary and unhealthy. It's OK to have the "blues." You probably need to slow down, let your soul catch up with you, or readjust to difficult conditions.

The person struggling with mild depression, however, can avoid a full-scale tumble into the chilling fog of clinical depression. Hundreds of psychologists around the world, through intensive scientific research, are discovering what the Bible has always told us: You feel what you think. Or, as the Bible says: "As [a person] thinketh in his heart, so is he" (Prov. 23:7, KJV). How we *think* about our problems will either relieve depression or aggravate it.

Pessimism is the core of depressed thinking. It is a risk factor for depression, just as smoking is a risk factor for lung cancer. Negative thoughts about the future, oneself, and the world stem from how we explain bad events.

When Sara broke up with her boyfriend, for example, it was her thoughts that drove her toward the precipice of severe depression. She felt the breakup was *permanent* ("It's always going to be like this"), *pervasive* ("It's going to undermine every aspect of my life"), and *personal* ("It's my fault").

The difference between people who pass through an episode of depression as quick as a rain squall and people who suffer for two weeks or more is usually simple. The latter group imagines the worst. They see their problems as permanent, pervasive, and personal. Those who bounce back after having the psychological wind knocked out of them see the bad event in the least threatening light. They see their problem as a challenge that is temporary and surmountable. Literally hundreds of studies show that pessimists give up more easily and get depressed more often.

Pessimistic prophecies are self-fulfilling. Repeating self-denigrating statements such as "I'll never be happy again" or "It's just not worth it anymore" lead to negative changes in mood. Pessimistic habits of thinking transform mere setbacks into disasters.

Optimistic thinking, on the other hand, can have the opposite effect. Paul understood this when he said, "Be transformed by the renewing of your mind" (Rom. 12:2), and "Be made new in the attitude of your minds" (Eph. 4:23). Paul encourages us to think about things that are true, noble, right, pure, lovely, admirable, and excellent (see Phil. 4:8). The words "think," "thought," and "mind" are used more than 300 times in the Scriptures.

Pessimism *is* escapable. The key is an optimistic personal dialogue. Think and say:

- "Just because I failed does not mean I will always fail or that I am a failure. Success is doing my best."

- "My pain is temporary. I may feel sad right now, but I'll bounce back."
- "I can rely on God for stability even when other relationships crumble. I will find love again."

Positive self-statements not only counter the effects of the negative thoughts that accompany depression but also energize us to take more control over our problems. Changing our attitude from pessimism to optimism helps relieve depression.

However, there is a point at which the blues cross a serious line. When a person is losing his or her grip on life, experiencing painful and incapacitating emotions, becoming ineffective in work or destructive in relationships, the time for professional help has clearly arrived.

Depression that is extremely deep, lasts more than a month, or that recurs often, should be treated by a clinical psychologist or psychiatrist. The sooner treatment of a severe depression is begun, the shorter its duration.

Whether we have the blues or "more than the blues," God is always available to help Christians through the healing process.

*I thank God for my handicaps, for through them,
I have found myself, my work, and my God.*

HELEN KELLER

**Yet man is born to trouble
as surely as sparks fly upward.**

JOB 5:7

BACKGROUND SCRIPTURE
Exod. 5:1; 8:19; Judg. 13—16;
Prov. 2:10; 4:23; 12:25; 13:12; 14:10, 30; 15:13, 15;
16:21, 23; 17:22; 23:6-7, 19; 27:19; 28:14; Phil. 4:8

5

Beliefs Affect Attitudes
by BILL O'CONNOR

HERE ARE THREE simple statements. It's permissible to argue with them, but I think they are three large stones in the foundation that shape our lives from beginning to end.

- "Thoughts are the seeds of beliefs."
- "Beliefs are the origins of attitudes."
- "Attitudes are the source of success or failure in life."

Those three statements can be summarized by the old maxim, "You are what you think." Cliché? Yes, but true! The Bible puts it this way: "Do not eat the bread of a selfish man . . . For as he thinks within himself, so he is" (Prov. 23:6-7, NASB).

How Attitudes Are Formed

I'm going to detail the formation of an attitude in five simple steps. Check me out by following a personal attitude (either a good one or a bad one) back to its roots. Prove whether I'm right or wrong.

Step 1: Some event occurs that has an impact on us. We like what happens, or we don't. The consequences of the event are either pleasant or unpleasant.

Bill O'Connor is ordained in the Church of the Nazarene. He is an evangelist, freelance writer, conference speaker, seminar leader, and founder of Northwest Christian Resource Service of Newberg, Oregon.

Step 2: We think about that event, and we tell ourselves certain things about it. It was a good thing, or it wasn't. It was fair or unfair. The person involved acted with kindness or with malice. We were treated well, or we weren't.

Step 3: What we say to ourselves affects how we feel about the event or circumstance. The circumstance may have been small enough at first to be almost neutral; but the more we talk to ourselves about it, the larger it becomes. Soon we begin to feel what we've been telling ourselves. What we feel may be positive: "He really likes me." "I really did a great job." "I'm very important to this company." Or what we feel may be negative: "I was cheated." "His actions weren't fair." "She treated me poorly." "I don't matter to these people."

Step 4: What we feel begins to manifest itself in our language. What we've been telling ourselves we begin to tell others. "This company isn't fair to its employees." "The boss doesn't care about us; all he's interested in is making a profit." "My wife doesn't really love me; she just needs me to bring home the paycheck." "Mom and Dad don't love me unless I get good grades." "My husband is a lazy, no-good slob."

Step 5: What we experience, think, feel strongly, and say out loud to others becomes a predominant attitude of life. When we dwell on all the negatives of life, our emotional, moral, and spiritual lives become clogged, like hardening of the arteries from a buildup of plaque. Our attitudes become hardened—negative and self-destructive. When we dwell on the positive, just like the surgery called angioplasty, which opens the arteries, our emotional, moral, and spiritual lives are expanded. Our attitudes become open—positive and personally healing.

Attitudes Are the Product of Beliefs

What we believe about life shapes our response to life. What we think and feel determines our belief system, and our belief system determines how we live. As a man or woman, boy or girl, thinks on the inside, so he or she becomes on the outside. That's God's own truth. If, for instance, life has "conspired against me" (an interpretation), and "everything has gone wrong" (another interpretation), I will begin to feel worthless, unhappy, and persecuted. Once those feelings become dominant, guess how I will act? That's right, I will act in a manner that reflects my interpretation of my worth. I will manifest unhappiness, and I will let everyone know how poorly I've been treated.

I have a cat. Like most humans, her moods are apparent. I think I can tell how she feels by looking at her or by listening to her. The biggest difference between us is that she's not as adept at hiding her feelings as some of us are. She can't mask her true feelings behind a smiling, self-confident facade. She can't pretend. We've become masters of pretense—but only temporarily. Once feelings and beliefs harden into attitudes, they cannot remain hidden long.

Why does a cat hiss, raise her back, and point her tail high in the air? Because she is scared. Or angry. Or upset. Why does she yowl? Because she's hungry. Or mad. Or wants attention. Her mannerisms and vocal responses are reflective of her feelings.

Why does a cat purr, which is something most cats do most of the time? Because the cat has a happy heart. She is content. Happy. Satisfied. Pleased with life.

Years ago I was a youth pastor. A set of identical twins in our youth group mirrored the two pictures I've just painted. One was like a discontented cat. She was grumpy, negative, critical, and unhappy. The other was like a contented cat. She was cheerful, positive, pleasant, and happy. I couldn't tell the difference between them physically; but let either one open her mouth, and I could tell instantly. Time would also tell. Within five minutes of entering the room, attitude made it obvious which girl was present.

The amazing thing, of course, was that two girls with identical physical attributes, raised in the same home with all of the same advantages and disadvantages, could turn out to be so different. It was easy to conclude that it was neither environment nor heredity that shaped these two divergent outlooks on life—it was choice.

It's an Issue of Choice

We can choose what we think about life and how we respond to life's circumstances. Our choices determine what we tell ourselves. What we tell ourselves determines how we feel, what we say, and how we act. Choice emerges as attitude.

Take Pharaoh, for instance, when Moses came to him saying, "Let my people go" (Exod. 5:1). He thought about it. He probably told himself he was being treated unfairly. After all, these people were his slaves. They had been his slaves since the day he was born. What right did they have to demand freedom? We can't trace Pharaoh's thoughts and feelings, but the Bible does tell us the result: "Pharaoh's heart was hard and he would not listen" (Exod. 8:19). What he thought and what he told himself affected his beliefs. His beliefs affected his emotions. His emotions determined his verbal response. And he was stuck with a destructive attitude. It was Pharaoh's *choice* that did him in.

Infants are born without either beliefs or attitudes, except for a love of self, which life can quickly take away. Each of us, as an infant, is a moral, emotional, and spiritual vacuum waiting to be filled. We're waiting for input. That input helps determine—for the rest of our lives—how we think and feel, and, as a result, how we respond. In short, life's input, and what we believe about it, shapes our attitudes.

Beliefs—and consequently the attitudes that spring from our beliefs—are shaped by a number of factors. Parents are our first influence. What they tell us. How they treat us. The names they give us or call us. The way they respond to us emotionally. All this input tells us who we are, how to feel about ourselves, and how we will respond to life.

In a supermarket I came across a mother pleading with her son to behave. He was out of control, and she was distraught. "Johnny," she said, "why are you acting like this?"

Johnny's reply was classic: "I'm not doing anything wrong, Mommy; I'm just being the little demon that you always tell me I am." Johnny's mother had labeled him. He thought about it, believed the label, then acted out his belief.

A long parade of people follow our parents: brothers and sisters, other relatives, neighborhood friends, teachers, schoolmates, pastors and Sunday School teachers, teenage peers, and fellow workers. Each of these persons tell us things about ourselves. They treat us in certain ways, tell us who we are, and how we ought to think. They attempt to build their belief system into our lives. We choose which pieces of this multitude of input we will accept and believe. Our choice affects who we become, how we think, how we speak, and how we act.

We grow up examining, testing, and adopting one belief after another. The process of maturing is a process of choosing and adopting beliefs as our own. Every choice we make helps determine a future attitude. We choose our attitudes by choosing our beliefs.

A Faulty Belief System Produces Destructive Attitudes

Another girl in my youth group was quiet and reclusive. She was socially insecure. Her only friends were other timid girls. Her shyness stemmed from a basic belief that was untrue: "I'm not pretty." I don't know where she got the false belief, and it really doesn't matter. Her problem was not the truth or untruth of what she believed, but the fact that she believed it. She was more attractive than 90 percent of the other girls in the group. Any boy would have given a week's pay to take her on a date, but she never gave them the opportunity. She told herself that she was unattractive, she believed it, and she conducted her life according to her belief. Her future—until she changed her belief about herself—was a tragedy in the making.

The Bible is filled with examples of beliefs resulting in attitudes that led to good or bad results. Samson is perhaps the classic example. (See Judg. 13—16.) He forgot who was the Source of his power, got to thinking of himself as pretty hot stuff, and ended up with the most costly haircut in history.

Here is what the Bible says in Proverbs about beliefs and their result:

- "An anxious heart weighs a man down, but a kind word cheers him up" (12:25).
- "Hope deferred makes the heart sick, but a longing fulfilled is a tree of life" (13:12).
- "Each heart knows its own bitterness, and no one else can share its joy" (14:10).
- "A heart at peace gives life to the body, but envy rots the bones" (14:30).
- "A happy heart makes the face cheerful, but heartache crushes the spirit" (15:13).
- "All the days of the oppressed are wretched, but the cheerful heart has a continual feast" (15:15).
- "A cheerful heart is good medicine, but a crushed spirit dries up the bones" (17:22).
- "Blessed is the man who always fears the LORD, but he who hardens his heart falls into trouble" (28:14).

What makes a heart cheerful? What makes a heart sick? What crushes a heart? What determines whether a heart is at peace or at war? What leads to life-crushing heartaches? Why do hearts become bitter?

We do all of those things to ourselves! We choose what we believe; our belief determines the response of the heart. If our choices are bad, so are our beliefs. If our beliefs are wrong, so are our feelings. If our feelings are negative, negative attitudes are seldom far behind. The Book of Proverbs also makes these truths clear:

- "The wise in heart are called discerning, and pleasant words promote instruction" (16:21).

- "A wise man's heart guides his mouth, and his lips promote instruction" (16:23).

A Realistic Belief System Produces Healthy Attitudes

I am not advocating we develop into a generation of Pollyannas who have lost touch with reality. That is not the desired product of appropriate response to circumstances and correct thinking about life. Rather, our goal is persons who can see the good among the bad, who can find the positive and make it the object of their thoughts. Such people generate positive beliefs, which lead to positive attitudes. That's why Paul penned: "Whatever is true, whatever is noble, whatever is right, whatever is pure, whatever is lovely, whatever is admirable—if anything is excellent or praiseworthy—think about such things" (Phil. 4:8).

We've all met them. People whose lives reflect the positive thoughts and beliefs that they consciously harbor every day. They're folks who have every reason to be unhappy—but aren't. Persons to whom life has handed nothing but trouble, but who aren't bitter or negative. People who have been mistreated but aren't jealous, angry, resentful, or bitter. People who have had none of the breaks but who have made something of life anyway. They did it because they believed they should.

We've also met the other kind. People who have every reason to be happy—but aren't. People who have responded negatively to circumstances. They have become twisted, unhappy, miserable folks whose company no one enjoys. Life's troubles have turned them sour, shaped their lives into a continual, distasteful pucker as if they had sucked a lemon. They're like that because they believe that's the way they have a right to be.

Choose Thoughts, Choose Beliefs, Choose Attitudes

What we're discussing here has many different names:

- Shad Helmstetter calls it "positive self-talk."
- Stephen Covey calls it "proactive language."
- Napoleon Hill calls it "conscious autosuggestion."
- Norman Vincent Peale called it "the power of positive thinking."
- Robert Schuller calls it "possibility thinking."

They're all talking about the same thing. What we say to ourselves repeatedly shapes what we believe. What we believe shapes how we feel about life. How we feel toward life shapes the way we talk and the way we walk.

The Book of Proverbs is once more a source of wisdom when it comes to the shaping of our beliefs.

- "For wisdom will enter your heart, and knowledge will be pleasant to your soul" (2:10).
- "Above all else, guard your heart, for it is the well-spring of life" (4:23).
- "Listen, my son, and be wise, and keep your heart on the right path" (23:19).

The wise man summed up the matter of belief and attitude when he penned: "As water reflects a face, so a man's heart reflects the man" (Prov. 27:19).

It's true, our beliefs affect our attitudes. Watch out! Think clearly. Choose wisely. Believe realistically and honestly. Talk positively. Tell ourselves the truth about life. *What we believe is what we become!*

As we wake or sleep,
we grow strong or we grow weak,
and at last some crisis shows us
what we have become.

BISHOP WESTCOTT

Therefore, since Christ suffered in his body,
arm yourselves also with the same attitude,
because he who has suffered in his body
is done with sin.

1 PET. 4:1

BACKGROUND SCRIPTURE
Ps. 116:1-9, 15

6

Choices in Crisis
by CAROLYN LUNN

ALL I COULD FOCUS ON was the pain—the unrelenting, excruciating, throbbing pain in my head. As I gradually came more and more to consciousness, I realized that though the most intense pain was in my head, my whole body was hurting. I'd never felt such pain. My first impulse was to try and move my arms and legs. I did move them, but it hurt.

What Is Going On?

My eyelids seemed too heavy to lift, so I tried to figure out where I was by the sounds around me. The disembodied voice on the paging system calling the names of doctors, the clanking sounds of carts moving down the hall, and the muffled sound of conversation. I realized I was in a hospital. Struggling to think, I tried to concentrate enough to put the pieces together. I gathered from conversation around me that they believed I was gravely injured. I felt the gathering shackles of fear.

It was late afternoon. The sun was low in the sky, and the shadow from the branches of the tree outside my window was

Carolyn Lunn is a wife, mother, grandmother, speaker, and author who lives in Olathe, Kansas. The above chapter is adapted from Mrs. Lunn's book, *Joy . . . Anyway.* Used by permission of Beacon Hill Press of Kansas City, copyright 1992.

silhouetted against the wall. I had regained consciousness and looked around the room. I was alone now. My heart was heavy, but I didn't know why. My mind was not able to think logically, to piece together why I was there. It was so hard to stay awake. I heard someone walking into the room, and I opened my eyes to see a white-coated doctor and another, shorter man.

My head hurt so badly, I could hardly focus my eyes on them. I felt a deep sense of foreboding as I waited to see what the doctor had to say.

"Carolyn," he said, "this is a pastor from a local church. He has come to see you.

"You are no doubt wondering what has happened," he continued. "At 4:30 this morning, you were in an automobile accident. You were brought to this hospital. You are in Hannibal, Missouri. You have been unconscious most of the day. You have been asking about your husband, and we know you are distressed about him. Carolyn, he was killed in that accident."

Awful black emptiness washed over me. Pain seemed to rip my heart apart. As darkness slowly began to envelop me, I heard the pastor begin to pray. I never heard the prayer's conclusion.

The Quick Trip

My thoughts went back to the time when we had begun to plan the trip to see my parents in Peoria, Illinois.

My husband, David, was a seminary student in Kansas City. It was August, and he was preparing for his middler year in the coming September. In the spring semester of his first year at seminary, he had been elected to serve as the editor of the seminary newspaper, and he was looking forward to this responsibility. This was one thing he and his friend, Duane*, had in common. They both loved to write and had served together on the school paper in college.

David was just finishing a summer school course. We had married in December of his first year in seminary, so we had only been married eight months. He was 22 and I was 20. We were excited about our preparations for the ministry. As a student pastor, he had accepted the pastorate of a small church in Oregon, Missouri. On the weekends we climbed into our little, chrome-less Chevy and drove the 90 miles to Oregon. We called in the community on Saturdays, held a morning and evening service on Sundays, and drove back to Kansas City to be ready for Monday. Still in the honeymoon stage of our life, we dreamed of the ministry we would have together.

David wanted to go to Peoria to see my parents. My father is a minister, and at that time was serving in the Illinois area. There was some theological unrest among some of David's friends who were students at the seminary, and he wanted to talk to my father about it. We were going to take a "quick" trip. We would leave Kansas City at midnight, spend all of Saturday with my parents, and travel back to Missouri all night to get to our little church in Oregon for the Sunday services.

I wasn't very excited about taking that kind of a trip and asked David why we couldn't wait until a time when we would be able to spend more time there. He explained that if we would go at that time, we would be able to ride with Duane, as he was going to Chicago and would simply drop us off in Peoria. This would help us financially, so we decided to go.

Before we started out to meet Duane that night, Dave came to the door of our bedroom and told me he was going to get some gas in our car. When he returned, we packed our bags in the car and started off. We were going to drive as far as Cameron, Missouri, in our car and leave it there in a church parking lot, and then ride the rest of the way with Duane. It would make it easier for us when we returned and needed to go to Oregon. Just after we had gone a few miles, Dave touched my shoulder and said, "Honey, come over close to me and pray for our trip tonight."

I can remember clearly praying and ending with the phrase, "Lord, if it would be Your will, please give us a safe trip and protect us along the way." This prayer would haunt me later as I tried to deal with Dave's death.

A Shattering Moment

In the early morning hours the three of us stopped at a little roadside café for a cup of coffee and a doughnut. When we came out of the store, Dave said, "Carolyn, why don't you get in the backseat and sleep so that when we get to Peoria, at least one of us will be coherent enough to visit with your folks right away."

We had both been sitting in the front with Duane, who was driving, so I slipped into the backseat. They were having an animated theological discussion; and I was sitting in the center of the backseat, holding a pillow in my arms and listening intently.

The last thing I remember is coming up behind two tractor-trailer trucks. As our friend decided to pass them, I was nervous because it was raining; and we were going fast on a blacktopped highway. I can remember that after we passed them, I felt a sense of relief. In the early morning darkness, the lights of the truck behind us illuminated the whole inside of our car. I remember no more. The events after that I learned from others.

After we passed the two trucks, for some reason, Duane put his foot on the brake. When he did, the car swerved around on the wet blacktop and crossed into the oncoming lane. A station wagon with eight passengers hit with tremendous impact on the passenger's side of our car. Three people were killed—the driver of the station wagon, a baby held in its mother's arms in the front seat, and David.

When I learned the details of what happened, I knew Duane would be blaming himself and suffering for it. I chose to visit Duane as I was leaving the hospital. As I entered the room, I could see he had suffered a severe leg injury, and one of his arms had been badly injured. His face was bruised and swollen. When he saw me, intense emotion was reflected in his eyes as he struggled with tears. Our feelings were so much on the surface it was hard to verbalize what we felt. In halting fashion, I told him that I harbored no bitterness. I will never forget his last words: "I only wish it had been me."

These words spawned my own questions: Why had my life been spared? Dave was the one who was going to preach. He was the tremendous writer. His was the ministry around which our lives were focused. He had such a gift of communication; my goals in life had been wrapped around his. *O God*, I echoed Duane in my aching heart, *it should have been me!*

I searched my heart and faced the truth that I had not grown in my relationship with the Lord as I could have. Dave had experienced a wonderful time of spiritual renewal and commitment a few months before he died. But I had depended on his strong faith, his spiritual leadership and vitality, and his prayer life to provide the sustenance for my own faith. I hadn't nurtured my own relationship with God. I had been so wrapped up with Dave and our ministry and the goals we were working toward, that when he was gone, the lack of depth of my own spiritual foundation was revealed.

God did not condemn me in those heart-wrenching moments. He created a deep, burning hunger in my heart. From my innermost being I prayed. I asked His forgiveness for my lukewarm heart, for being willing to live vicariously through the faith of another, instead of continuing to forge my own path with Him. I acknowledged my own helplessness—and He heard my prayer.

Life Would Never Be the Same

Even as I dealt with my grief, it still didn't seem real. Dave's death had been so sudden. Almost from the time I had been told, I had felt that unless I attended the funeral, I would not grasp the finality of it all.

When we arrived in Columbus, Ohio, I asked to go immediately to the funeral home. As I entered the room at the mortuary, my heart pounded. When I saw David's body, the reality of his death ripped through me. He was gone. I reached out and touched his hand. He would never hold me in his arms again. He would never smile that mischievous sideways grin of his and tease me with gentle relentlessness. We would never again sit and talk for hours, learning to know each other.

The day of the funeral I was aware of all that was happening. I could see and hear, but the pain was blessedly numbed. When the service was over and the final moments arrived, the unshakable reality of the moment pierced the protective shield. Life would never be the same. Once again I felt deep emptiness and grief.

Often during those days that followed, Dave's family and I looked at old photographs and reminisced. It helped all of us to talk about Dave. I was the last one to be with him before his death, and we needed each other.

Return to the Scene

Soon the time came to go back to Kansas City. We stopped in Cameron, Missouri, at the church where Dave and I had parked our car. It sat in the same place, covered with a two-and-a-half-week coat of dust. No one had touched it. I wanted to be the first one to touch it now. As I got in the car, a lump rose in my throat. I drove the car the rest of the way to Kansas City. It was something of Dave's that I could have with me all the time.

In Kansas City we had several stops to make—closing our accounts at the bank, picking up a glossy Dave had ordered for speaking engagements, meeting with a lawyer about legal matters, packing our belongings.

As we finished each task, I knew I was closing a door on that chapter of my life. The finality of it hit me everywhere I turned. At times, my grief was so intense, I had to find some quiet place alone, a place where I could pour out my tears and heartache to Jesus. I needed the sense of His presence to go on, and each time He comforted me with His peace.

One particular incident seems to best illustrate my feelings. On the trip back to my parents' home we stopped at a restaurant. I was self-conscious, because my face was still bruised and discolored. As quickly as possible, I sat down. After we had ordered, I looked around the restaurant at the people gathered there. When I had entered the restaurant, some had stared at my face, but now they were quietly conversing and carrying on with the details of their lives. It had seemed for just one moment they had acknowledged the trauma of my life and shared it with me. But now it was forgotten.

How can you people sit there and so nonchalantly go on with your lives? I wanted to shout! *Don't you realize what has happened? My husband is dead! He'll never know the stages of life you take so for granted. Can't you feel my pain? Don't you know my life will never be the same again? For one moment there it seemed you were aware, but now . . .*

That's when it hurts so badly—when everyone picks up the pattern of their lives, but there is no pattern to yours at all.

No Money-back Guarantee

When we arrived in Peoria, my world was shaken once again. My father had received a phone call from David's insurance agent. The agent asked if we knew that the insurance company had received the death certificate and already paid the claim for the policy. Because the cause of death was accidental, double the amount had been paid. The payment had been claimed by and paid to Dave's parents.

Upon hearing the news, my mind flashed back to an evening about two weeks before Dave's death. He was working at his desk and called me over to discuss our finances. He showed me insurance forms for a life insurance policy he'd purchased while he was a student in college. The beneficiaries were his parents, but he was filling out a new form, making me the beneficiary. He pointed out the death benefit and the double payment clause. Then he told me that his parents had carried two small insurance policies on him also from the time of his birth and that he knew if anything happened to him, they would want me to have the money. Dave went on to explain the financing of our car. He told me about the glossy photo he'd had taken and when it would be ready. "The only other bill we have is for a couple of suits in the cleaners," he said. He concluded by telling me how much money was in our checking and savings accounts at the bank.

I was disturbed that he was being so specific about this, and I told him so. He explained that he didn't want me to worry about how I would make it if something happened to him. "Honey, if something should happen to me," he said, "I want you to finish your education."

I wondered after Dave's death if he had a premonition that he should get those papers done and explain our affairs. But Dave hadn't sent the new beneficiary insurance forms in before the accident.

My father spoke to Dave's father, who felt that Dave wanted them to have the money because they had raised him, and he had only been married to me for eight months. They felt entitled to keep it. I was devastated. This was the money that would pay for my education.

Suddenly it seemed as though I was aware of the presence of God saturating that room. He'd been there all the time, ready to meet my need. I wasn't alone. I wasn't powerless. I wasn't without resources. I did not need to be afraid of the future. He was already there. In that instant, when resentment and bitterness were digging their way to take root in my heart, I cried out to God. Desperately I told Him I couldn't handle anything more.

Often in the years since, I have struggled with these same feelings in other situations. I have wanted God to heal me instantly. But God does not always heal instantly. Sometimes the healing comes just as surely, but slowly, as He works His heal-ing balm in our lives. But He *does* heal!

A Different Point of View

In the quietness of my parents' home I confessed my inad-equacy to bring healing in this situation. I asked God for wis-dom. I reminded Him of how often I have spoken when I should have been silent, how I have not always said the heal-ing thing in threatening situations. I have retaliated with quick words. I surrendered my tongue and my mind to Him, *knowing* I would fail unless His power and love were able to freely flow through me.

I tried to see the situation from Dave's parents' point of view. For one thing, they were nearing retirement and were probably anxious about their finances. Second, their life focus had been on Dave's ministry and dreams for his future. This money was their last link with their son.

Extreme stress or trauma can make any of us respond in ways that are not normal to our personality. I believe this was the case with Dave's father. He was not the same man after Dave died. He had always been a kind man, respected and loved by his children. This was not a normal reaction for him. His grief caused him to react in ways not consistent with his personality.

I have learned that in crisis times we cannot program how another person will react, or how long it will take them to deal with the emotions brought on by the crisis. It is helpful to be sensitive to the dynamics in these situations. We should be careful what we say and do. Because of our own intense emo-tions, we are apt to retaliate. Oh, how we need to cling to God in times like these!

A Different Approach

Asking God to help me choose the timing and to prepare their hearts for my request, I called Dave's parents and asked them if they would loan me half of the money they received from the insurance company to help me pay for my education. I told them I would pay them back on a regular basis as quickly as I was able. They agreed to the loan, and I was grateful—for I had an emotional attachment to its link with Dave. It was that money he had talked about as a provision for my education, and now it would be so.

In the following years Dave's family and I worked diligently to keep our relationship one of love and caring. I drove from school in Illinois to see them in Ohio for weekends. They came to the school to share with me in some of the special moments in my life. Our love for each other deepened during those years. The loan never had to be repaid. That picture in the corridor of my mind has lost its power to ravage me. The sting is gone!

David's father died a few years later, still carrying a deep sense of grief for his son. Later David's mother died. She called me from the hospital to tell me she was very ill. In a voice so faint I could hardly hear it, she told me she could not love me any more if I had been her own child.

At her funeral, as I sat with the family, I was filled with awe and wonder at the way in which God had answered my prayer that day in my parents' home. I had no regrets and no "if onlys" because of the mighty power of a merciful God who is in the healing business. His desire is to heal the hurts of each of us in a far greater measure than we could ask or think!

---

*Not his real name.

*The final test of a leader
is that he leaves behind him in other men
the conviction and the will to carry on.*

WALTER LIPPMANN

*I will declare your name to my brothers;
in the congregation I will praise you.*

PS. 22:22

BACKGROUND SCRIPTURE
Num. 13; Ps. 78:11; Matt. 4:19; 16:18;
John 14:12; Acts 1:8; 2:42-47;
1 Cor. 1:4-5; 11:2

7

Groups Have Attitudes Too

by DANN SPADER and GARY MAYSE

EVERY GROUP, every club, every church, and every ministry has an image of itself. In fact, every person within a group has his or her own version of that image. Churches are no exception. Stop for a moment—what are the first thoughts that come to mind when we think of our church? Those thoughts are a part of our group image. That image may be positive, exciting, frustrating, depressing, or anything in between.

A healthy group image is directly connected to our effectiveness in helping people grow as disciples of Christ. It is a major part of a nurturing environment. We need to recognize that our group image will either contribute to or hinder the impact of ministry.

A Healthy Group Image in Action

Under the inspiration of the Holy Spirit, Luke recorded the events of the Early Church. In so doing, he also gave us insights into the dynamics at work behind those historic events. Acts 2:42-47 has long been recognized as a summary statement of life in the Early Church. We see at least four insights into the image the early Christians held of that Church.

This chapter is reprinted from the book *Growing a Healthy Church*, by Dann Spader and Gary Mayse. Used by permission of Moody Press, Chicago, copyright 1991.

● **They were devoted** (v. 42).

The people were devoted and committed to one another as well as to the ministry and mission of the Church. They had bound their hearts together for the duration. It was long-term devotion. Needless to say, that level of commitment happens in direct proportion to a general enthusiasm for the cause.

● **They were together with oneness** (vv. 44, 46).

Their spiritual unity was demonstrated by the way they were continually meeting together. People who are not enthusiastic about a group do not frequently go out of their way to participate in it. Yet those early Christians met together daily in the Temple, in their homes, for study, and for meals. They were inseparable.

● **There was a sense of gladness** (vv. 46-47).

Luke tells us that there was an overwhelmingly positive attitude among these believers. Sincere gladness and praise flowed freely whenever they gathered together.

● **They enjoyed the favor of all the people** (v. 47).

Perhaps most instructive of all is this final phrase. The image of this Early Church was so healthy that it made an impact on those outside the Church.

The Impact of a Healthy Group Image

Some will react to this idea of building a healthy group image with skepticism. "Just preach the Word," they might say. Preaching the Word is foundational, but it is not the only task of the Church of Christ. The Early Church had an explosive impact on the world, and Acts 2 demonstrates the link between the healthy dynamics of that body and its impact. The impact of our group image will be felt in at least three other crucial areas.

● **Teachability**

Stated in the first person, this principle is: "The more excited I am about the group, the more receptive I am to the things I learn there." The truth of this principle is borne out when members of a church attend a retreat or seminar. They leave with a great attitude and come back raving about the profound influence it made on their lives.

A professor of communications and a specialist on the implications for Christian ministry has done much research on this subject. From his study he has discovered that when the health of a group's self-image is increased, the people of that group become more eager, receptive, and responsive as learners.*

On the contrary, when people hold a low view of their group, they hold a low view of the things taught there. The higher the group image, the more open people are to the teaching. This can be seen when people come expecting significant results from services and Bible studies. A healthy group image changes the way people feel about being there. And naturally, if people are eager to participate, they are more enthused about inviting others.

- **Outreach orientation**

The higher the image people have of their church, the more willing they will be to bring others. Conversely, the lower their image of the group, the greater their resistance to reaching out to others.

It makes sense. When a person regards something highly, he or she is proud to belong and comfortable recommending it to a friend. However, when uncertain or negative about the ministry, he or she won't recommend it for fear of being embarrassed and ashamed.

- **Commitment to the cause**

In addition to the impact on teachability and outreach orientation, a healthy group image has a direct bearing on the level of tangible commitment. Commitment is often expressed in a list of stewardship issues. For example, how often do urgent needs for workers and finances arise? And how often are these needs publicly discussed in guilt-laden tones? Such unmet needs are possibly the result of a poor group image. Furthermore, the hammer of guilt will only compound the problem if a poor group image is responsible.

When people believe in the ministry, their tangible commitment will follow naturally. That commitment is often demonstrated by increased giving and greater personal involvement.

We Cannot Not Communicate

Researchers in the field of communication have long discussed the fact that more than 50 percent of the messages we send are communicated nonverbally. Body language and tone of voice communicate more than words. That means the things we feel are observed by others, regardless of what we say or do not say. People read our nonverbal language; hence we cannot *not* communicate.

No one would dare say that changing a group's attitude is easy. Doing so is accomplished much as any other change, beginning at the fountain of new life—on our knees. Pouring our hearts out to the Lord, we can ask Him to bring about the growth and change needed.

The three practices that follow are powerful tools for encouraging a healthy outlook. In many ways they will put feet to our prayers. They will make a noticeable difference.

Parade the Potential, Not the Problems

Scripture is filled with examples of people who had reasons to be discouraged but were not consumed by them. When confronted by problems, they focused on the potential. In spite of drastic situations, they identified assurances of hope. If we do the same, our perspective will be elevated to greater health. And as we do so, the health of the group's image will grow dramatically.

Paul's letters to the Christians in Corinth make clear that church had more than its share of troubles. There were factions, confusions, sinful behavior, and more. Yet he still found reason to praise them. He elevated their potential, not the problems: "I always thank God for you because of his grace given you in Christ Jesus. For in him you have been enriched in every way" (1 Cor. 1:4-5). "I praise you for remembering me in everything and for holding to the teachings, just as I passed them on to you" (11:2).

When Moses sent the spies to check out the Promised Land, Joshua and Caleb saw the same sights as the other 10 spies. They saw the obstacles, and they felt the sway of public opinion back home. Yet they publicly defended a different perspective. What had they seen differently? While the 10 were noticing how big the sons of Anak were, Joshua and Caleb were remembering how big their God was.

A classic story has been told about two young boys who were identical twins. From birth they were impossible to tell apart, except for one feature. One boy was always negative, whereas the other was always positive. As a result the boys were taken through a series of psychological tests. Their discoveries were predictable.

The doctors decided to try something a bit out of the ordinary. They took the generally happy boy and placed him in a room devoid of everything but a large pile of manure heaped up in the center of the floor. After telling him to wait for them there, the researchers left the room.

Within a matter of moments everyone heard the boy whooping and hollering at the top of his lungs. Afraid something might be wrong, they all rushed back to see what was the matter. They found the boy on top of the manure pile, scooping up handfuls and throwing it everywhere. In spite of the odor, he was in boyish ecstasy.

The doctors asked the obvious question. "Son, what on earth are you so excited about?"

The boy answered, "With all this manure, there has to be a pony in here somewhere!"

Clarify and Communicate Vision

A healthy group image is not just a collective experience of "warm fuzzies." Rather, it is a tangible enthusiasm about the work God is currently doing and the work He wants to do in the future. Just as the word "enthusiasm" literally means "God in us," a healthy group image is built upon His active presence.

Developing the ability to verbalize vision—that purpose or driving passion God has given—can be a powerful tool. A clearly communicated vision connects purpose with conviction, provides substance to enthusiasm, and fuels godly dreaming—all of which contribute to a healthy group image.

What has God called us and our church to do? Can we crystallize it into a memorable sentence? Put it in words so that it might be communicated. Clarifying and communicating the vision God has given gives people ownership in the fact that He has called us together for a specific purpose.

Jesus cultivated and confirmed His vision for His disciples in many ways. The Great Commission expressed it most succinctly, but all along the way He had set the stage. Listen to the following examples, and consider what an impact they must have made on the disciples.

- "Come, follow me . . . and I will make you fishers of men" (Matt. 4:19).
- "On this rock I will build my church, and the gates of Hades will not overcome it" (Matt. 16:18).
- "I tell you the truth, anyone who has faith in me will do what I have been doing. He will do even greater things than these, because I am going to the Father" (John 14:12).
- "But you will receive power when the Holy Spirit comes on you; and you will be my witnesses in Jerusalem, and in all Judea and Samaria, and to the ends of the earth" (Acts 1:8).

From His initial invitation until His final words to them, Jesus communicated to His disciples that He had great plans for their lives. He had dreams and purpose for them. He believed in—He counted on—the potential of their ministry.

But many churches have such a watered-down, generic sense

of purpose, it's no wonder people aren't excited. In some cases, the vision some hold is nothing more than the vague notion of being "the church," as in, "Our church exists to be a church!"

Celebrate the Way God Has Worked

One final thought about building a healthy group image: celebrate the good times! This is one of the simplest and most easily workable ideas. Whenever something good happens in the congregation, review it publicly with the whole body.

Most of us have selective memory. We remember in detail those things that went wrong, and we forget the details about the things that went well. Reviewing the good times can help counteract this tendency. Remembering is so important in Scripture that a theology of remembrance could easily be constructed. Over and over again God tells His people to remember what He has done and how far they have come. Elaborate memorials were constructed. Many of the feasts are designed specifically to assist the remembering process.

Biblically speaking, God's desire is to provoke healthy remembrance of the good times in general and His specific works. In Ps. 78, God makes clear that the Israelites lost perspective spiritually because they did not remember His works. "They forgot what he had done, the wonders he had shown them" (v. 11).

Our group image might well be suffering from selective memory. Perhaps the lack of enthusiasm has been created by a forgetfulness about God's work in the past. Therefore, celebrate—continually review—the good times in any and every way possible.

At this point some people in difficult circumstances might be tempted to cry, "How can we celebrate the way God has been working when God is not working in our church!" Even in the most trying situations, the task is to discern how God is working. It is certain that He is at work, for if God were not working, He would be dead.

A healthy group image will affect every area of ministry. In one sense it will feed everything we do. In another sense it will be fed by everything we do. Building a healthy group image can be one of the most enjoyable tasks. Everyone likes to be the bearer of good news!

---

*Em Griffin, *The Mindchangers* (Wheaton, Ill.: Tyndale, 1976), 202. See also sections titled "Mold," chaps. 8—11.

*Christianity does not remove you
from the world and its problems;
it makes you fit to live in it,
triumphantly and usefully.*

CHARLES TEMPLETON

*May God himself, the God of peace,
sanctify you through and through.
May your whole spirit, soul and body
be kept blameless at the
coming of our Lord Jesus Christ.*

1 THESS. 5:23

BACKGROUND SCRIPTURE
Matt. 17:17; 19:19; Luke 10:40; 16:1-8; 22:44;
Acts 11:1-18; 13:4-5; 15:39; Rom. 12:1;
2 Cor. 12:7-9; Phil. 4:11; 1 Thess. 3:5; 1 Tim. 6:6;
2 Tim. 1:5-6; 4:11; 1 Pet. 2:1

8

Sanctification and Attitudes

by LEON and MILDRED CHAMBERS

OFTEN IN OUR DAILY lives we confuse sin and human nature. We wonder about attitudes that we have or hear others express. We ask, "If I am sanctified, am I sinning if I feel this way?" Or we wonder, "If that person is sanctified, how can he or she have such an attitude?" Often our confusion arises because we are not clear about what sanctification changes in our lives and what it does not.

Some would make the experience of sanctification mean too little. Others, however, would insist upon a perfection that would rob us of our humanity. The experiences of conversion and sanctification deal with the sin problem in the human life but do not affect normal human conduct. The Holy Spirit works *through* human weaknesses or infirmities; He does not *eliminate* them.

Errors in Judgment

The experience of holiness does not mean that we will not

Mildred Chambers is a graduate of Trevecca Nazarene College and has a Ph.D. from George Peabody College for Teachers. Her husband, Leon Chambers, is an ordained elder in the Church of the Nazarene and a graduate of Trevecca Nazarene College and Nazarene Theological Seminary. He has a doctor of education degree from the University of Southern Mississippi. This chapter was adapted from *Holiness and Human Nature,* © 1975, Beacon Hill Press of Kansas City.

err in judgment. The perfection required is perfection of motives, not perfection of the intellect. In Acts 11:2 (KJV), the apostles and brethren "contended" (that is, "differed") with Peter over his eating with the Gentiles. Peter explained that he was directed by a revelation from God to eat, preach, and pray with the Gentiles. Then the same apostles and brethren "praised God, saying, 'So then, God has granted even the Gentiles repentance unto life'" (v. 18). The brethren erred, but they had not sinned. Their contention would have hindered the Church, but there was no rebellion against the known will of God. When light came, they walked in it.

Such obedience keeps us sinless and guiltless even when there are errors in judgment that result in misunderstanding. These errors may be stumbling blocks to the one who errs and to others as well. It is possible that they could even keep some unsaved person out of the Kingdom. But there is no sin or guilt in mistakes and errors in judgment. As long as we are not rebellious, are walking in the light and obedient, we are fully accepted children of God.

To say that we Christians who err in judgment have not sinned is not to say that we may be indifferent and will not need to improve. We will lament, grieve, and pray over the errors. While they are not held against us as sins, such mistakes will prevent us being as effective Christians as we might be.

Lack of Harmony

The experience of holiness does not mean that there will always be perfect harmony among the Spirit-filled. Paul and Barnabas were "sent on their way by the Holy Spirit" on the first missionary journey (Acts 13:4). At a place called Salamis "John [Mark] was with them as their helper" (v. 5). Later, however, Paul refused to take Mark on a second missionary journey. "They had such a sharp disagreement that they parted company" (15:39).

The division was not sin; it was human. There is no evidence of any unkind, ulterior motives. In fact, when Mark later proved himself, Paul wrote, "Only Luke is with me. Get Mark and bring him with you, because he is helpful to me in my ministry" (2 Tim. 4:11). Paul did not let differences cut off fellowship.

There is no sin in misunderstandings and differences of opinions. There *may* be sin in our attitude concerning them.

Physical Perfection

Holiness does not insure physical perfection. Records of suffering saints and accounts of prayers for healing that go unanswered fill the pages of Christian literature. Dedicated men and women weep because physical limitations keep them from achieving for God as they wish they could.

Paul experienced such a problem. "To keep me from becoming conceited because of these surpassingly great revelations, there was given me a thorn in my flesh, a messenger of Satan, to torment me. Three times I pleaded with the Lord to take it away from me. But he said to me, 'My grace is sufficient for you, for my power is made perfect in weakness'" (2 Cor. 12:7-9). God did not deliver Paul from his physical problem, but He did promise grace to bear it. God also said that He would be glorified as Paul bore his weakness.

The sanctified person has a body that shows the effects of the fall of Adam and Eve in the Garden of Eden. This body tires, falls prey to diseases, at times functions with difficulty. It may take great physical effort to carry on our work for the Lord. The fact that special effort is required is not a sin. We need not feel guilty. God understands our humanity. Sanctification does not give an extra supply of energy; it does not make us superhuman.

Perfection of Works

Holiness does not mean perfection of works or self-discipline. As sanctified persons, we will not necessarily perform perfectly each time we have an opportunity to work for the Lord. Humanity prevents this. In 2 Tim. 1:5, Paul expressed deep appreciation for Timothy's faith: "I have been reminded of your sincere faith." Paul is speaking of Timothy's faithfulness to God, but immediately he gives an admonition: "Fan into flame the gift of God, which is in you" (v. 6). Even with Timothy's faithfulness, he could improve his service.

It is human to have shortcomings. But it is Christian to press on, to seek God's grace, and to try to overcome these frailties of humanity.

Temptation

Holiness does not place us beyond temptation. When we are saved, our sins are forgiven. However, our experiences of our past sinful life are recorded on the brain in permanent "memory traces." Scientists have discovered that when areas of the brain are electronically stimulated, past experiences can be revived with all the reality of reliving them. In everyday living a sanctified person will remember past experiences under certain circumstances.

If our sins are forgiven and our hearts are sanctified wholly, memories of the past may be a source of temptation but not sin. The past may be a battleground, but it does not have to be defeat.

Negative Emotions

Holiness does not place us beyond the possibility of experiencing negative emotions such as hurt feelings, impatience, worry, anxiety, and similar emotions. To feel an emotion, even strong emotion, is not sin within itself; it is human. We must know the motive behind the emotion to determine its purity or sinfulness. The motive (or attitude) is an internal state that is the cause of behavior. Values and goals are products of our motives. Attitudes determine the behavior involved in reaching a particular goal.

Emotions can help us enjoy or dislike a task. They facilitate or impede learning. They influence our interpretation of another person's behavior, either positively or negatively. While unbridled emotions can erode our spiritual life to the point that they can become sin, they need not do so. We need a well-developed, well-balanced emotional life in order to be normal persons.

We differ in our emotional responses. All people are emotional, but no two are alike. A recognition of individual differences is necessary, or we will stumble in our understanding of perfect love. These individual differences are genetically and environmentally based.

Paul seemed to have no problem in preaching to the Gentiles, while Peter required a special revelation. Barnabas had no problem in forgiving Mark, while Paul required Mark to prove himself. This would say to us that some people find it easier to forgive and forget than do others. Some people just seem to be nice by nature, while others seem to have trouble even with the help of the Holy Spirit.

Since people differ so greatly in emotional responses, and since emotions can be evaluated only on the basis of the underlying motives, we would do well to judge no one. To get red in the face cannot be equated with hostile motives, as is so often thought. A person might react quickly, speak sharply, and even flush; but these responses may be the result of humiliation, threat to security, fear, or embarrassment rather than anger. Another person might become pale in response to the same stimulus.

The sanctified may even experience strong emotions. Jesus experienced some kind of strong emotion in Gethsemane. Luke 22:44 speaks of Christ "being in anguish." The original Greek shows the word *anguish* to mean "a conflict or struggle." The agony referred to was mental. It was more than mere physical pain.

Whether a strong emotion is sinful depends upon what

occasioned it and how it is handled. It must be kept in mind that emotions may lead to sin if they result in loss of faith in God, if a person's motives are affected to the point of rebelling against God.

Let's take a look at some specific emotions.

Concern. Concern may be defined as caring about something. It is considered a somewhat mild emotion. Everyone would agree as to the place of concern in daily living. Christ in His parable of the unjust steward recognized the legitimate place of concern. The unjust steward was commended and told that those who are concerned and plan for the future are wise (Luke 16:1-8).

Worry. Worry is considered by many authorities to be a mild response to fear. Worry is a common emotion, closely related to anxiety but more mild. This emotion is characterized by a circular thought pattern. The worrier in preoccupation thinks over the problem again and again. Worrying breeds more worry. Fear provokes worry, and worry provokes more fear.

Worry in itself is not sin. Paul was so disturbed (worried) concerning the state of the church at Thessalonica that he could not rest until Timothy was sent to investigate and returned with a good report. Paul said, "When I could stand it no longer, I sent to find out about your faith. I was afraid that in some way . . . our efforts might have been useless" (1 Thess. 3:5).

Worry may result from the guilt we feel because of sins committed. But for the Christian whose sins are forgiven, the fears that underlie the worry are not based upon actual guilt. Therefore the worry is not sin.

Death is our enemy. It is normal to fear death. A sanctified man may be told that he has a terminal illness. He might go through a period of preoccupation with this problem based upon fear. He might be said to "worry" about the condition. He has not sinned. Naturally, in proportion to the degree that he is able to rise above the fear, worry diminishes.

Anxiety. Anxiety is a strong emotion of apprehension or uneasiness stemming from threat or danger, the source of which may be unidentifiable. In this sense it differs from fear in that the latter is attached to an identifiable object or event in the environment. As with any aroused state, the physiology of the body is altered, the extent of alteration depending upon the degree of anxiety.

For example, the nerves may be so reactive as to be "on edge," causing us to respond out of proportion to the stimulus. We may jump at the slightest noise. The heart and the breathing rate may accelerate; digestion may slow down or speed up; and even the skin may respond with flushing, pallor, or sweating. All these are automatic reactions when we feel threatened, just like anxiety.

Jesus probably experienced some form of anxiety when He actually faced the "cup." His physiological reaction was sweating, as Luke describes it, "like drops of blood falling to the ground" (Luke 22:44). Yet Christ did not sin. Once again, sin involves rebellion. A sanctified person who feels threatened may respond with anxiety but without sin.

Impatience. The sanctified may experience impatience. Impatience is the lack of endurance or long-suffering. Our patience threshold is affected by fatigue, illness, stress, or pressure. In these states, we respond more quickly, are more sensitive to a greater variety of provocations, have less emotional control. A sick or tired person is not a "normal" person. Even though sanctified, our physical endurance and, specifically, nervous endurance are limited.

If impatience is a sin, any degree of the emotion is a sin, even impatience with oneself, which all sanctified have experienced—even if under some other label. Some would seem to think it is all right to be impatient with oneself, but not with others. This is inconsistent. Impatience within itself is not a sin.

Even Jesus grew weary of faithlessness and expressed it strongly: "O unbelieving and perverse generation . . . how long shall I stay with you?" (Matt. 17:17). Patience is a fruit of the Spirit. All the Spirit-filled have the fruit of the Spirit, but not all Christians bear all of the fruit equally. There are degrees of spiritual maturity among the sanctified.

Discontentment. The sanctified may suffer discontentment. This emotion may be constructive in that it may move us to higher levels of action. On the other hand, it may be detrimental when we become preoccupied and can't see beyond our circumstances.

The opposite of discontentment is contentment. Paul said, "For I have learned to be content whatever the circumstances" (Phil. 4:11). Note the word "learned." Contentment does not come automatically with sanctification—that is, not constant contentment with all things. While discontent within itself is not a sin, the sanctified should *learn* contentment. "But godliness with contentment is great gain" (1 Tim. 6:6).

The foregoing discussion of emotions has tried to show the place of such common emotions as anxiety, worry, impatience, and other emotions in the life of the sanctified. The purpose is not to "whittle out" a loophole to let us crawl through, settle down, and enjoy or indulge such emotions. The purpose is to help the sanctified avoid self-condemnation for normal, human conduct. Such condemnation can be detrimental to our spiritual victory.

Remember, we have not sinned as long as our motives are pure and there is no rebellion. Any behavior that is an outgrowth of a sinful motive is sin, whether it be an outward act or an internal emotion. But where the motive is pure, the behavior—whether an outward act or an internal emotion—is not sin.

Certainly, emotions may lead to sin. If the emotion affects our Christian faith to the point that we become rebellious, then the motive is no longer pure. Our goals are set according to our motives. When a motive becomes sinful, then sinful goals will be chosen. Sinful motives and sinful goals result in sinful acts. Thus, emotions may lead to sin.

For example, Martha wanted Jesus to rebuke Mary in order to get her assistance when she was "distracted" with her household tasks (Luke 10:40). Jesus did not treat Martha's action as a sin. If Martha had indulged her emotions to the point that she wanted Mary humiliated and embarrassed, then Martha's motives would have been changed, her goal would have changed, and Martha would have been guilty of sin. Her emotions would have been based upon sinful motives and, as such, would have been classified as sinful.

Even when emotions are not sin, they can hinder our fruitfulness and can be a stumbling block to us and others. Peter's emotion of fear of the Jews, which separated him from the Gentiles, made him a stumbling block to the Gentiles. They must have wondered why he ate with them one day and would not eat with them the next. But his fear was not sin.

Sanctification does not change the biology of the nervous system, which is basically responsible for the physical aspects of emotions; but sanctification does purify our motives. Sanctification will help us see the need to strive to develop the emotional control that is possible within the limits of our physical bodies.

The experience of holiness does not prevent us from experiencing strong feeling, but it will save us from being unkind or trying to hurt or get even. Holiness will not keep us from desiring fair play, but it will enable us to carry on even if not being treated fairly. The sanctified person may at times experience hurt, embarrassment, humiliation, or similar emotions; but, by the help of the Holy Spirit, we will walk in the light, return good for evil, and serve God with all our hearts.

The question that we might well ask is whether we really love God with all our hearts and love everyone else as ourselves. If we can honestly answer yes, then we need feel no condemnation.

Maturity

Holiness does not bring instant maturity. When we are

first saved and sanctified, we are just as Christian as the one who is mature in Christ; but we are still infants in Christ.

Peter gives incentive to young Christians. "Like newborn babies, crave pure spiritual milk, so that by it you may grow up in your salvation" (1 Pet. 2:2). At the moment of conversion, spiritual learning begins. The infant in Christ, by the help of the Holy Spirit and the Church, must shape new behavioral patterns.

Faulty emotional training, unscriptural beliefs, wrong concepts of faith, the development of a falsely guilty conscience, and many other problems may trouble us throughout our earthly journeys. When we are filled with the Holy Spirit, there is greater impetus to grow. However, when newly sanctified, we have only the potential for spiritual growth. Growth is the development of a lifetime. It is not achieved instantaneously.

Biological Drives

Holiness does not abolish biological drives. A majority of the textbooks list hunger, thirst, sleep, and sex among the numerous biological drives. There is no sin in any of these drives. All are necessary for the welfare of the individual and the propagation of the race. There is sin in certain types of behavior in response to the physiological pressures induced by the drives. But there is a Christian way to meet all of the biological drives.

The sanctified will seek to see, taste, smell, and touch what will be to the glory of God, even though we will be tempted to do otherwise. The sanctified will not seek to be aroused for evil.

This was Paul's admonition in Rom. 12:1: "Offer your bodies as living sacrifices, holy and pleasing to God." The whole body is on the altar to be used to the glory of God. The drives are not eliminated from the sanctified, but they are kept pure.

Self-love

The experience of sanctification does not bring an end to loving oneself. It has often been preached that we should not love ourselves. The Bible is very clear that as Christians we will love ourselves. In fact, we cannot be a biblical Christian if we do not love self. "Love your neighbor as *yourself*" (Matt. 19:19, emphasis added). Jesus teaches that love for self is the standard for treatment of others.

Acceptance of self will largely determine our attitudes and behavior toward others. If we have a good self-concept, we will have reason to be at peace with ourselves and with others. We feel significant in the sight of God. We have accepted what we can and cannot do. This will bring peace.

The Christian is in the best possible position to love self and to love others. We can face God without guilt and face ourselves and others without condemnation. There is no need to strike out at others nor to blame them. Christian love for self is not selfish, not conceited. It is mentally healthy. Christian love is peace with self and with others. A Christian who feels truly loved of God will love himself or herself.

As long as we remain confused about sanctification and human nature, we will not be able to grow spiritually and develop mature attitudes. The experiences of conversion and sanctification solve the sin problem but do not obliterate our normal, human conduct or eliminate infirmities. God does promise that the Holy Spirit will help us with these human weaknesses, and that is an attitude that allows us to grow in the Spirit-filled life.

*I can forgive, but I cannot forget, is only
another way of saying, I will not forgive.
Forgiveness ought to be like a canceled note—
torn in two, and burned up, so that
it never can be shown against one.*

—HENRY WARD BEECHER

*For if you forgive men when they sin against
you, your heavenly Father will also forgive you.
But if you do not forgive men their sins,
your Father will not forgive your sins.*

MATT. 6:14-15

BACKGROUND SCRIPTURE
Ps. 32:3; Matt. 6:14-15; 9:1-8; 1 Pet. 3:9

9

Releasing Bad Attitudes

by DAVID G. BENNER

SOME PEOPLE GET STUCK in their anger because they confuse expressing anger with releasing it. Expression of any feeling is almost always a necessary first step to releasing it, but expression and release are not the same thing. In expressing my anger, I continue to embrace it. It is *my* anger, and for a while I may even feel glad that it is mine. It feels good to be angry. I am, at this stage, usually very aware that I am not giving it up, just expressing it.

As I am using the phrase, "releasing" the anger means giving it up. It means letting go of my right to revenge. It is forgiving other people for what they did to me. And this act of forgiveness, properly understood, is perhaps the most difficult thing a human being can ever be asked to do.

Forgiveness: The Hard Work Miracle

With forgiveness, we do our part; and then we ask God to do His part. His part is in helping us release the anger and then in giving us the resulting emotional freedom and healing. I don't simply pray to God that He will render the other person

David G. Benner, Ph.D., is a clinical psychologist and university professor. This chapter is reprinted from his book, *Healing Emotional Wounds.* Used by permission of Baker Book House, copyright 1990.

forgiven by me. Unfortunately, it is not that easy. I can and should pray that God would help me forgive the other person. This is a prayer He will answer because it is clearly something that He wills for me.

Note the relationship between receiving forgiveness and giving it. As it is hard to imagine how one could ever give love if he or she had never received love from another, so it is hard to imagine how someone could forgive another if he or she had never received forgiveness. Knowing myself to be one who has needed and received forgiveness allows me to grant others this great and undeserved gift. And supremely, knowing myself to have needed and received the forgiveness of God allows me to become a forgiving person in a way that is quite impossible when only dealing with the experience of forgiveness as received from the hands of fellow humans.

The Importance of Forgiveness

The overriding emphasis forgiveness receives in Scripture makes it a most important concept in Christianity. Throughout both Old and New Testaments we are presented with the supreme value of divine forgiveness of our sins and are repeatedly enjoined to forgive others for their sins against us. Jesus linked these two expressions of forgiveness to each other by declaring, "For if you forgive men when they sin against you, your heavenly Father will also forgive you. But if you do not forgive men their sins, your Father will not forgive your sins" (Matt. 6:14-15). It would be hard to imagine how Jesus could have given the importance of forgiveness any more emphasis than this.

The process of confession, repentance, and forgiveness is at the core of the Christian model of healing of our alienation from both God and each other. But forgiveness involves even more than the healing of our relationships. Scripture also presents evidence for a link between forgiveness and health. David spoke of how his "bones wasted away through [his] groaning" until he finally confessed his sins and received God's forgiveness (Ps. 32:3). Jesus also demonstrated the close connection between forgiveness and physical health in His cure of the paralytic who was healed as a result of His forgiving his sins (Matt. 9:1-8).

This close connection between forgiveness and health has recently also been noted by medical researchers. Recent research has shown that people who have a tendency to hold resentment and a related inability to forgive others are much more likely to develop both cancer[1] and heart disease.[2] An even more direct risk to physical life has been noted by psychiatrist E. Mansell Pattison, who suggests that murder typifies the ultimate failure to forgive another and suicide the ultimate failure to forgive oneself.[3] A failure to forgive others, and the accompanying resentment and bitterness, has also been reported to be the leading cause of burnout.[4]

The Problem of Premature Forgiveness

People often try to forgive others before they know that for which they are forgiving. They usually have not yet really allowed themselves to feel the hurt and are using forgiveness as a way to defend against the pain. The preparation necessary for genuine forgiveness includes the two stages of reexperiencing the emotions and reinterpreting the hurt. There are no shortcuts to this process of preparation.

The problem is that premature attempts at forgiveness seriously obstruct the emotional and intellectual work of the earlier stages. If I believe I have already forgiven the other person, why should I explore the hurt and express the feelings? The truth is that I cannot really forgive another until I know the feelings I am releasing. And by "know" I do not mean mere intellectual understanding. I also mean the experiential knowing that results from the work of the first two stages of emotional healing.

The Forgiveness Process

Forgiveness is the capstone to the healing process. There

is no simple, cookbook approach to forgiveness. There are, however, some steps that, if followed, increase the chances of success in forgiveness. I will describe four such steps.

● **Understanding resistance to forgiveness**

Seldom are we ready to release the pain of a significant hurt until we understand why everything within us resists such a step. One frequent reason for resistance to forgiveness is that I may feel it is my *right* to hold a grudge. In the experience of hurt my rights were trampled. Now I am going to stand on my rights, and it only seems fair to conclude that I have a right to be angry. But accepting anger as a natural response to hurt is not the same as accepting it as a right. Standing on my right to hold a grudge is standing on dangerous ground. It is running the risks of chronic bitterness.

Another reason for my resistance to forgiveness is often that I may not yet be ready to give up the sense of power I feel over the person who hurt me. This is best understood by recalling the powerlessness that I experienced in the first stages of hurt. At that point I felt weak, vulnerable, and helpless. But my anger has now restored a sense of power to me, and I may be reluctant to give this up.

A related source of resistance may be my reluctance to give up the feelings of moral superiority I now enjoy in relation to the person who hurt me. My wound may have been the occasion for the development of a victim role, and I may now be exploiting this role as I nurse a feeling of smug condescension based on moral superiority. Such feelings are also very difficult to relinquish.

Sometimes I resist forgiveness because I equate my withholding of forgiveness with the punishment of people who hurt me. It is quite clear to me that such people deserve to be punished for what they did to me. It may, in fact, be accurate to conclude that they should be punished. However, the fallacy in this line of reasoning is the assumption that I am the one to do this and that I do so by withholding forgiveness. Vengeance and ultimate justice belong to God. They are His responsibility. Furthermore, while withholding forgiveness does indeed inflict punishment, this punishment is inflicted not on the other person but on myself. I must, therefore, give up the idea that it is my responsibility to punish people who hurt me and that I do so by withholding my forgiveness of them.

Another reason why I may resist forgiveness is that I may feel I can only forgive other people if they request it. I may feel that other people need to come groveling to me, expressing sorrow and regret for their actions, and offering restitution and promises that they will never hurt me again. But is this really necessary for forgiveness?

I do not believe that it is. If it were, we could never forgive a person who was dead, and we would be bound to the emotional consequences of hurt for the rest of our lives. My forgiveness is not dependent on any response from other people.

A variant of this source of resistance is feeling that I can only forgive other people if they deserve it. This may take the form of not letting them off the hook until they have "learned their lesson." Under the mantle of these apparently noble intentions, I conclude that my withholding of forgiveness is in their best interest—not for their punishment, but for their learning. I may judge that if I forgive them, they will not continue to reflect on their misdeeds. I, therefore, set up some hoops through which they must jump before I am willing to forgive them.

This way of viewing forgiveness reflects the same sort of moral superiority described earlier. In such a view, forgiveness must be earned. But in reality, forgiveness is always unmerited. If people can do something to earn my forgiveness, they don't need it. Forgiveness has its meaning in the grace of God. His forgiveness of us is always a gracious and extravagant response to us. There is nothing I can do to earn God's forgiveness, and there is nothing another can do to earn mine. Freely we have received, freely we must give.

A final reason for my resistance to forgiveness is that it makes me vulnerable once again. In the experience of hurt I felt vulnerable, exposed, and raw. In such circumstances it is common to seek protection, either by means of retreat or aggression. When I once again begin to experience some sense of safety, I am very reluctant to leave it. Everything within me recoils from taking steps that will lead me toward further vulnerability.

That is quite understandable. In fact, it is the most realistic of the sources of resistance we have considered. Forgiveness does involve risk, and risk involves vulnerability. The major risk of forgiveness is that of further hurt. It often hurts even more when I am hurt a second or third time by someone I have previously forgiven.

But while there are risks to forgiveness, there are also risks to withholding forgiveness. And these risks are even greater. The risk of being unforgiving is a life of chronic bitterness and hatred. We noted earlier that this is a terminal condition, one that involves the destruction of body, soul, and spirit. The chances of damage to ourselves from withholding forgiveness are extremely high. We must, therefore, be careful to never underestimate these risks. The chances of a subsequent hurt at the hands of the one who hurt me are not to be ignored but are usually lower than the chances of hurt to myself if I withhold forgiveness. On this basis I would suggest that forgiveness is always the better risk.

● **Clarifying misunderstandings of forgiveness**

The second step in forgiving someone is to make sure that my understanding of forgiveness is accurate. Misunderstandings of forgiveness are common, probably due in part to the fact that the concept is such a popular one. However, if these misunderstandings guide our efforts at forgiveness, we will inevitably fail in our efforts and will bog down in the feelings of hurt and anger.

To forgive is not to forget. Not only is the adage "forgive and forget" misleading in the suggested ease with which it characterizes the action involved, but also it is seriously mis-leading as to the outcome.

To forget a hurt is to repress it. Forgiveness does not elim-inate memory. Acts that have been forgiven are still available for recall. However, over time they should have less and less emotional pain attached to them. The goal is remembering without feeling malice. This is the sign that forgiveness has completed its healing work.

To forgive is not to excuse. A second common misunder-standing of forgiveness assumes that it involves excusing the behavior of the one who hurt me. If I can excuse the behavior, forgiveness is unnecessary. But, on the other hand, it is precise-ly because the behavior of the one who hurt me is so inexcus-able that I must forgive. Forgiveness is the only healing re-sponse to such injustice.

There are always reasons why other people behave as they do, and sometimes these reasons will even make sense to us if we come to know them. However, reasons are not the same as excuses. There are reasons for everything we do in life, but some of what we do is still inexcusable. To make excuses for the other person is to engage in rationalization as a way of de-fending against the hurt. But in most instances of serious hurt, the behavior that hurt us is genuinely inexcusable.

To forgive is not to ignore. Attempts to ignore pain and hurt are sometimes also confused with forgiveness. In such situa-tions I attempt to ignore the feelings of hurt or even the person who hurt me.

But this is also not forgiveness. Forgiveness does not in-volve overlooking the offense. It involves facing it head-on. It requires thinking about the hurt and the one who hurt me. It involves accepting the experience as real, not attempting to minimize it. The hurt must be accepted as a part of reality. To ignore or to overlook it is an attempt to change reality by the power of selective attention. Such magical thinking does not produce genuine inner healing.

To forgive is not necessarily to extend unconditional trust. A final misunderstanding of forgiveness involves the assumption that if I have forgiven people who hurt me, I should now be able to extend to them unconditional trust. Forgiveness, in such a view, is only complete if I can treat the other person as if the incident of hurt never happened.

This is really a variant on forgiveness as forgetting. It assumes that after the act of forgiveness, I can act as if I don't remember what happened. This is impossible. We will remember, and we must act in the light of that memory if we are to be responsible to ourselves and to the other person. Genuine forgiveness means that I no longer hold the hurt over the head of the other person. To do so would be malice. It does not mean that I must assume that I will never again be hurt by that person, nor does it mean that I should never take steps to minimize this possibility.

In some circumstances I may sense the other person's genuine remorse and conclude that I can safely extend complete trust without guarding myself further against recurring hurt. This assumption may turn out to be incorrect, but the choice is still usually the right one in the absence of a pattern of past behavior such as that which hurt me. It is better to occasionally be naive and be hurt a second time by someone than to be so untrusting as to never allow those who hurt me access to me again. However, in other situations caution and limited trust may be the most appropriate way of dealing with the person. Even so, my inability to extend unconditional trust does not mean that I have not genuinely forgiven the other person.

Think, for example, of a person who repeatedly steals things from you every time you invite him to your home. Or, an even more powerful illustration would be a baby-sitter who sexually abused your children. In such circumstances you would be called to forgive these people for these actions, but such forgiveness would not demand that you continue to offer them access to your home or to your children.

Similarly, people who repeatedly violate a trust of confidence should not be given further confidences. Or someone who repeatedly lies should not be given responsibility that would allow that lack of truthfulness to continue to hurt others. Forgiveness sometimes means that I will still have to be cautious around the one who hurt me. Unconditional trust is neither a necessary consequence nor an indication of forgiveness.

True Forgiveness

If true forgiveness is none of these things, what is it? Most simply, forgiveness is letting go of my malice and my right to retaliate, and letting go of my right to hang on to the emotional consequences of the hurt. These are the things that I cling to as long as I refuse to forgive, and these are the things that in forgiveness I voluntarily choose to relinquish.

In forgiveness I give up the claim I feel I have on the one who hurts me. I consider the account to be balanced. Anything I felt myself to be able to hold over the other person I now relinquish. Forgiveness is not repaying evil for evil or insult for insult, but giving a blessing instead (1 Pet. 3:9). It is wishing others well; it is praying that God will bless them and facing them in love, not hate. It is giving up my malice.

True forgiveness also involves relinquishing the emotional consequences of the hurt. I may continue to feel anger, hurt, depression, or other such consequences, but I choose to no longer embrace them. They are not my right. They are things that I now seek to leave behind me. Recurring waves of pain remind me that healing is not yet complete, but they are not to be savored in self-pity. Rather, they are to be released as quickly as I can.

This is what we see in Jesus' prayer of forgiveness from the Cross. His plea to His Father to forgive those who crucified Him because they did not know what they were doing expressed His own forgiveness of them as well as His realization that, in their ignorance, remorse was unrealistic. They were not about to feel sorry for that which they were doing, but this fact did not stop Jesus from forgiving them.

Complete and perfect forgiveness is available to all of us through God. My own offerings of forgiveness need not be limited by my past experiences of forgiveness. God's forgiveness of me can serve as both a model and as a source for my own forgiveness of others. I am not dependent on having had forgiving parents or experiences with young and forgiving children. A perfect Heavenly Father stands ready and willing to forgive me each time I come to Him requesting such forgiveness. And then, freely having received, I can more freely give.

1. S. Achterberg, S. Matthews, and O. C. Simonton, "Psychology of the Exceptional Cancer Patient," *Psychotherapy: Theory, Research, and Practice* 6 (21): 13-14.

2. Redford Williams, *The Trusting Heart: Great News About Type A Behavior* (New York: Random House, 1989).

3. E. M. Pattison, "On the Failure to Forgive or to Be Forgiven," *American Journal of Psychotherapy* 31 (1): 106-15.

4. F. Minirth et al., *How to Beat Burnout* (Chicago: Moody Press, 1986).

*Though all afflictions are evils in themselves,
yet they are good for us, because they discover
to us our disease and tend to our cure.*

JOHN TILLOTSON

*Is any one of you in trouble? He should pray.
Is anyone happy? Let him sing songs of praise.*

JAMES 5:13

BACKGROUND SCRIPTURE
Mark 5:25-34; 10:46-52; Luke 17:11-19; Rom. 5:1-11;
Phil. 1:18-20; 1 John 2:28

10

Activities That Mask Attitudes

by PAUL FITZGERALD

STEVE* COULD NOT LET HIMSELF fall asleep. More worried than tired, he asked himself, "Why did this happen again? I've got too much to do. Why didn't I just say no?" It was a pattern he despised in himself. Had he not promised his family it wouldn't happen again? He could have declined his pastor's request to mow the church lawn; but he did live near the church, and he did have a riding mower. His wife was upset. It was happening again. The family was being sacrificed after he had promised to spend quality time with the family.

They agreed that he would call the pastor, but he could not bring himself to go to the telephone. He was stuck between his desire to be more involved in the family and the compulsive need to please everyone else. Finally, it was midnight. Steve slipped out of bed, careful to not awaken his wife. He pulled on old jeans and thought to himself, "Good thing the church lawn is well lit. I can be back in bed by three and still get some sleep before the alarm clock rings."

In another household the mail was depressing Sara.* Nothing but bills, bills, bills. Lately, there were too many to handle. "If only some unexpected checks would show up, we could get some relief," she thought. Just six months earlier

---

Dr. Paul Fitzgerald is a counselor and pastor in Somerset, Kentucky, and specializes in working with Christian recovery groups.

they celebrated the last payment of a consolidation loan. They were trying to keep their commitment to pay their tithe. Sara realized what had happened. The long months of struggling to pay off the debt had been depressing. It had felt so good to finally buy the new clothes the family needed. Yet they were heading around the vicious circle of budgeting, sacrificing, feeling depressed, spending to feel better, then becoming more depressed. Sara wondered about a way out but succumbed to the familiar empty feeling inside. Intending only to rest a minute with coffee and a doughnut, her next awareness was of having eaten every doughnut in the box. She did not like what had happened, but at least that empty feeling was gone.

Steve's overcommitting and Sara's overspending or overeating are common patterns found among both Christians and nonbelievers. Excessive talking to maintain control, compulsive gossiping, sleeping to avoid social contact, watching television to the neglect of responsibilities—any behavior obsessively or compulsively used to dull underlying feelings of low self-esteem, inadequacy, worry, fear, pain, or confusion can prevent healthy functioning. In extreme forms, these avoidance behaviors become addictive or predispose one to use substances addictively.

Compulsive Behaviors Are Destructive

Compulsive actions begin unconsciously as a means of avoiding feelings of powerlessness. Yet, we remain morally responsible for the consequences of our choices. The destructive results of behaviors can serve to warn us emotionally, physically, socially, and spiritually that something is vitally wrong. However, our denial defenses can totally cut off awareness of the painful results to ourselves and to others. We become blind to the information that would help us choose different and healthy responses to the underlying anxiety. Compulsive actions become unthinking and illogical responses any time unpleasant feelings arise, despite painful results. Relationships suffer. The nurture of loved ones is sacrificed for behaviors that falsely bring feelings of relief. Personal spiritual freedom is exchanged for rigidly focused, legalistic, and punitive spiritual bondage. Recent studies suggest that even religious choices can be used compulsively or addictively.

The Attitude Behind Compulsive Behaviors

People who use compulsive behaviors to cope with anxiety may present a picture of competence in other areas of their lives and appear to honestly express their feelings. Yet, behind this facade is the domination of fears linked by the common thread of shame:

- fear of being found out or exposed
- fear of being judged incompetent
- fear of failure
- fear of being ignored or abandoned
- fear of being imperfect
- fear of falling apart

Unfortunately, shame has not been significantly addressed by either religion or psychology. Instead, the dominant focus has been on guilt, sometimes labeling shame as "false guilt." It comes as a surprise to many that "shame" words (232 times in KJV; 304 in NIV) appear many more times in the Bible than do "guilt" words (KJV 33; NIV 196). While shame and guilt are related, they are distinctly different experiences requiring distinctly different responses for remedy.

Guilt Is Not Shame

Guilt results from having done something wrong; a complex set of feelings creating the fear of punishment. Awareness of guilt may come as surprisingly as red lights flashing in the rearview mirror and an officer asking, "Do you know how fast you were driving?" We experience guilt as the result of our actions that we judge to be legally, ethically, or morally wrong. The anxiety of guilt is the threat of being punished. Guilt is remedied by confession, restitution, forgiveness, or suffering punishment. By these means the guilty is made guiltless again.

Shame's anxiety is not a threat of punishment, but the fear of not being approved, of being disliked, or of being abandoned. Shame may accompany guilt for a wrong action. But shame is not so much having *done* wrong as it is a sense of *being* wrong—defective, dirty, or incompetent. To feel guilty is to acknowledge participation in something outside of me that was wrong. To be ashamed is the overwhelming feeling that "I am bad." Seeking forgiveness or suffering punishment does not remedy shame. Since God does not create defective souls, the prayer "Forgive me for being defective" is ineffective. Punishment, either from others or self-imposed, does not remedy shame.

Healthy Shame

Some of the confusion is that while being "guiltless" is good, being "shameless" is not good at all. Shamelessness impairs moral decision making and in extreme cases results in psychopathology, where a person can be horribly cruel with no compunction for the cruelty inflicted. Healthy shame is part of the human condition that reminds us we are not God and informs moral decision making.

Shame is experienced as a surprise, a sudden self-consciousness that is universally expressed in a blush, averted eye contact, slumped shoulders, and a desire to become so small as to be invisible. Biblical languages have several different words translated by English terms for shame: "dishonor," "disgrace," "embarrassment." Both the Hebrew and Greek languages use separate words for three distinct aspects of shame: (1) "sense of shame" that leads to making moral choices; (2) "disgrace" for actions inconsistent with moral values; and, (3) shame as a necessary precondition for "reverence" or "awe" before God. A healthy sense of shame is linked with healthy spirituality that allows one to both experience reverence and awe in the worship of God without danger of being abandoned. To have either too little shame or too much shame can impair our spirituality.

Like most trapped in compulsive behaviors and addictions, Steve and Sara had overwhelming feelings of guilt for their choices. They could no longer deny the pain their choices were inflicting on their families. Each of them often prayed to God for forgiveness and sought forgiveness from their families. But the compulsive power of fear and shame was not broken. If Steve was forgiven, what was still wrong? If Sara wasn't forgiven yet, what else did she need to do?

Internalized Shame

Shame is most destructive when it becomes the dominant self-description of a person. One author has written that shame is

the affect of indignity, of transgression, of alienation. Though terror speaks to life and death and distress makes the world a veil of tears, yet shame strikes deepest into the heart of man. While terror and distress hurt, they are wounds from the outside which penetrate the smooth surface of the ego, but shame is felt as an inner torment, a sickness of the soul. It does not matter whether the humiliated one has been shamed by derisive laughter or whether he mocks himself, in either event he feels himself naked, defeated, alienated, lacking dignity and worth.[1]

Prolonged exposure to sources of shame has toxic, long-term effects on how the shamed person views himself or herself. Shame becomes internalized as a persistent self-image of being powerless, incompetent, dirty, and lacking dignity. A shamed self-image is a colored lens before which all the events of life pass for evaluation and which screens out any contradiction that they deserve to be ashamed. Perfectionists see every flaw in their work where others claim to see none. Compliments are dismissed: "Anyone could have done it." Expressions of love are rejected: "If you really knew me, you could not love me." Each failure to live up to promised changes in behavior patterns results in more shame and reconfirms the shamed self-image. Hiding one's shamed self becomes life's priority, as exposure would risk abandonment and rejection.

Any experience of abuse, neglect, abandonment, overprotection, or overinvestment are shaming messages that become internalized with repetition. Steve describes his childhood as "normal." He was a good student and excelled at sports. However, his father worked long hours, often with a second job, to provide for the family, and that prevented him seeing most of Steve's games. Each of the children had chores that came before play. Steve still recalls his father's harshness over a missed chore: "You're never going to amount to anything if you can't keep a promise and do what you say you'll do."

Sara felt alone most of her life. An older sister seemed smarter and prettier when she got attention from the boys at school and church. Her brother seemed to always be in trouble at home and at school. Not wanting to be any trouble for her parents, Sara blended into the surroundings and stayed out of the way. She remembers with clarity a family vacation when her parents packed and left for home following her brother's defiance. But Sara was left in the motel pool! They returned for her when they realized she wasn't with them, but they laughed and tried to brush it aside. The pain of abandonment went undercover when her child-heart leaped with joy at seeing her parents return for her. Today her parents rarely visit her, choosing to spend their time with her sister and brother and their families.

Healing Internalized Shame

Overcoming some obsessive-compulsive behaviors and addictions may require the help of a professional counselor. In many cases churches, pastors, and friends can be sources of the grace needed for healing. God's grace includes both forgiveness for the guilt of sins and acceptance as one who is loved, valued, and affirmed. In Romans 5, Paul describes what shamed persons cannot hope to believe is possible. In verses 1-5 shame's anxiety, hopelessness, and feelings of deserved rejection are overwhelmed by the flood of God's love and the affirming presence of the Holy Spirit. Verses 6-8 remind us that the shame of being powerless to change sinful patterns is overcome by God's love that initiates undeserved forgiveness. And in verses 9-11 joyous reconciliation replaces the disgraceful feelings of having lost face before God experienced as "God's wrath." "Reconciliation" is the translation for an intensive, compound Greek word suggesting the thoroughness of the action. The change from being ashamed to unashamed includes a changed emotional outlook on life. Paul calls in verses 2 and 3 for rejoicing "in the hope of the glory of God" as well as "in our sufferings," sufferings that might otherwise have been a source of shame. "Rejoice" translates an intensive Greek word suggesting a bold confidence in God.

Paul claims motivation for ministry in his unashamed, confident rejoicing over reconciliation with God, not in shame-based compulsive choices. His desire is to continue freely choosing to follow Christ with "sufficient courage" despite the appearance of his imprisonment, which was a source of shame in the eyes of some believers (Phil. 1:18-20). This same connection of living free of toxic shame and having a confident, bold attitude is found in 1 John 2:28 as a desirable experience for all believers.

Jesus' death and resurrection are most often theologically connected to forgiveness for guilt. The Gospels also portray how Jesus responded to people shamed by circumstance and society—a beggar, a blind man, a woman sick for years. Consider the shame of the lepers—separated from family, living outside the community, having to call out their own shame to any who came near: "Stay away! I have leprosy!"

Jesus modeled a pattern for healing shame. First, the Scriptures tell us that He really looked at them and restored

their dignity. His eyes were not averted by their shameful circumstances. He restored their personal importance. Next, He
asked what they wanted Him to do for them. These social out-
casts were used to being told what to do and where to go, as if
they were incompetent. Yet Jesus, who knew what they needed, still asked them and empowered them to choose. Then, Jesus touched them lovingly. They had been rudely and inappro-
priately touched by many who wanted them out of the way
and out of sight. Jesus' healing touch made Him ceremonially
contaminated; He took their shame upon himself. But with His
touch they received the grace of unashamed acceptance.

Steve and Sara—and all of us—need insight about our
past shaming experiences and the impact on our present sense
of self. We need permission to establish boundaries to protect
ourselves from shaming patterns. In time we can find the grace
to forgive those who shamed us, but healing waits until we encounter someone who will be Jesus to us. Someone who will
look at us in nonshaming ways and invite us to expose our injured self. Someone who will empower us by listening to our
story and who will speak to us with dignity. Someone who will
honor personal boundaries but touch us in loving acceptance.

Would you be that person for me? Could I be that person
for you? Can our churches be healing places where the cap-
tives of shame are set free? Many churches of all sizes are finding that support groups and recovery ministries are effective
ways to provide healing for many who struggle with compulsive behaviors and addictions.

---

*Name has been changed.

1. Silvan S. Tomkins, *Affect, Imagery, and Consciousness: The Negative Affects*, vol.
2 (New York: Springer, 1963), 118.

The gem cannot be polished without friction,
nor man perfected without trials.

CHINESE PROVERB

I have told you these things,
so that in me you may have peace.
In this world you will have trouble.
But take heart! I have overcome the world.

JOHN 16:33

BACKGROUND SCRIPTURE
Matt. 7:3-5; 18:15; 23:13-33;
Rom. 12:18; Eph. 4:15, 25

Honest Communication

by BILL HYBELS

WHO SAID THE FOLLOWING harsh words?

"Woe to you, teachers of the law and Pharisees, you hypocrites!"

"You blind guides! You strain out a gnat but swallow a camel."

"You clean the outside of the cup and dish, but inside they are full of greed and self-indulgence."

"You are like whitewashed tombs, which look beautiful on the outside but on the inside are full of dead men's bones and everything unclean."

"You snakes! You brood of vipers! How will you escape being condemned to hell?"

Most people probably recognize these words of Jesus, the *gentle* Shepherd, the *tenderhearted, meek,* and *lowly* Savior! (See Matt. 23:13-33.) How could He talk so tough to people He claimed to love? Why did He say these hard words?

Jesus said these things because they were true. His words were upsetting, difficult to receive, tough to swallow—but true. Quite often the truth must simply be told straight out, with no room for confusion or misinterpretation, to avoid the

---

greater damage of living by lies. Jesus had an overwhelming concern for the people He was addressing. He loved them, and He wanted them to come to grips with the truth before they shipwrecked their lives and jeopardized eternity. Jesus was demonstrating *tough love*—a kind of love that is usually painful but very potent.

I've received my share of hard words over the years. There comes a time when the truth must be told, and it must be told straight. Fortunately, some people have loved me too much to allow me to continue to act in a rebellious, deceitful, or arrogant fashion. So they made me face some unpleasant things about myself that were damaging my character and jeopardizing our relationship. That's what I mean by tough love—and I love those people for using it on me.

Tender People and Tough Love

Tender love is badly needed in this hard-hearted world. We need compassion, sensitivity, affirmation, and encouragement. But without its counterpart, tough love, tender love can rapidly degenerate into a sniveling sentimentality that paves the way for deception and, eventually, the disintegration of the relationship.

To tenderhearted people, tough love sounds unnatural, frightening, and maybe even unchristian. Admittedly, it comes easier to those of us who are by nature tougher hearted. When we see a problem in the life of someone we love, we do not hesitate to go to work on it. We easily say, "What we need here is surgery. So let's lay this guy out, and with a scalpel or a dull butter knife—it doesn't matter which—let's hack through his surface-level excuses and get right to the heart of the matter. And if it causes a little bleeding, that's OK as long as the problem gets fixed. We'll stitch him back up later. If he survives the surgery, he'll thank us later."

Tenderhearted people who read the last paragraph already have their stomachs in their throats. They are saying to themselves, "Surgery? Scalpel? Blood? I never want to see that happen to anyone, let alone do it myself. All I want is peace and harmony. Maybe with enough hugs, the problems will solve themselves and the pain will go away." To tenderhearted people, I say, "I understand your tender spirit—God made you that way. But if you're going to learn how to really love, you're going to have to learn about tough love."

Who Needs Tough Love?

Everywhere I look I see people who need to experience tough love—precious people who really matter to God but who are running around in circles, dizzied by deception. I see married couples on the edge of serious trouble, young people pushing their luck to the limits, all kinds of people wandering aimlessly in the wastelands of destructive pleasure seeking. Too many of us who see these people destroying themselves simply chew our nails and wring our hands, saying nothing because we do not understand tough love.

But somebody has to get close to these people and tell them they're on a merry-go-round going nowhere. Somebody has to say, "I love you too much to watch you shipwreck your life, your marriage, your family, your job, your soul. So sit down and listen to me, because I'm going to say some hard things to you. I don't like doing this, but I must because these things are true and because I love you too much to stay silent when I see you hurting yourself."

In order to understand tough love and express it effectively, a person must have two fundamental convictions. First, he or she must believe that *truthtelling is more important than peacekeeping.* Second, he or she must realize that *the well-being of the other person is more important than the current comfort level in the relationship.*

Truth Telling or Peacekeeping

Tenderhearted people will go to unbelievable lengths to avoid any kind of turmoil, unrest, or upheaval in a relationship. If there's a little tension in the marriage and one partner asks the other, "What's wrong?" the tender one will answer, "Nothing." What he or she is really saying is this: "Something's wrong, but I don't want to make a scene." In choosing peacekeeping over truth telling, these people think they are being noble, but in reality they are making a bad choice. Whatever caused the tension will come back. The peace will get harder and harder to keep. A spirit of disappointment will start to flow through the peacekeeper's veins, leading first to anger, then to bitterness, and finally to hatred. Relationships can die while everything looks peaceful on the surface!

The Lord gives a command in Eph. 4:25 that makes tenderhearted people tremble to their bones: "Therefore each of you must put off falsehood and speak truthfully to his neighbor, for we are all members of one body." First, we are to stop lying to each other. Second, we are to speak the truth—in love. (See verse 15.) It takes courage to speak the truth when we know that doing so will make waves and rock canoes. But any approach other than truth telling, over time, will undermine the integrity of our relationships. A relationship built on peacekeeping won't last. Tough love chooses truth telling over peacekeeping and trusts God for the outcome.

Counterfeit Peace

In the early years of our marriage, both Lynne and I chose peacekeeping over truth telling. I was starting up a church, and I had a lot of upheaval at work—no money, no people, no buildings, and plenty of disagreement among those who were involved with the project. Lynne had troubles of her own at home. She was pregnant. We had two boarders living with us who took a great deal of her time. And she was teaching flute lessons to help make ends meet. So with upheaval at home and upheaval at work, we had a common understanding whenever we got together—"Don't make any more waves." Nevertheless, inside us the frustrations were building.

God began to work on Lynne's heart. Before long, my tenderhearted wife started meeting me at the door, saying, "Sit down, I have to tell you something. I haven't been truthful with you. I am sick and tired of being 10th on your priority list. You don't show me much affection. I don't like the way this marriage is heading, and I'm not going to stand for it."

I did not respond very well. I did not say, "I'm glad to hear what's on your heart. I'll change my schedule and start thinking about your needs as well as my own." Instead I yelled, "With all the problems I have trying to start this church—and you lay this trip on me! What do you want, anyway? Here, take some blood!"

In spite of my reaction, Lynne stuck to her guns. She knew our marriage needed work, and she decided to speak up until I saw the light. Over the years God used Lynne's tough love until I faced the truth about myself and allowed Him to do a lot of surgery on me.

Once I started listening to Lynne and working on my problems, I began seeing some things in her I did not want to live with anymore. Having learned the value of truth telling, I decided to open up. "Sweetheart," I said, "I see a streak of self-centeredness in your life that bothers me."

Sweet, softhearted Lynne did not say, "Thank you for sharing your feelings." Instead she ran away sobbing, "I can't believe you'd say that!" and slammed the bedroom door. But I stuck to my guns, and we had several more rough months. Eventually she made some changes, just as I had to do, and our marriage became peaceful again. But this time was different. This was not a counterfeit peace based on avoiding the real issues. This was the peace of the Lord—based on truth, real, and lasting.

Well-being or Comfort

To love as Jesus loves, then, we have to put truth telling ahead of peacekeeping. We also have to put the other person's well-being ahead of the comfort level of our relationship.

One of the best definitions of tough love I know is *action for the well-being of the beloved.* We need more people who love others with such devotion that they will risk their current comfort level in the relationship and say whatever needs to be said in order to protect the other person's well-being.

I went to a close friend one time when I saw his life taking a bad turn. I took him to a restaurant and said, "I'm not trying to run your life, but I'm concerned about the direction it's taking." He was so angry that he came close to leaping over the table to punch my lights out. So, man of valor that I am, I looked him in the eye and said, "Sorry, I'll never mention this again." I didn't, either, and he shipwrecked his life. I still see this friend occasionally, and many times I've said to him, "I failed you. I should have been on you like a shirt. I should have said, 'Leap over that table and deck me if it will make you feel any better, but I'm going to tell you again that I'm concerned about your future.'" Maybe God would have used me if I had been a little more tenacious.

Whenever we take action on behalf of another person's well-being, we are taking a big risk. The comfort level may drop precipitously. Over time, however, the outcome of speaking the truth in love—especially when the relationship is basically mature and healthy—is usually positive. The obstacle in the relationship turns into a building block, and we reach new understandings, make new commitments, and establish deeper trust. But we all know that it is much easier to write and read about tough love than actually to sit down and have a heart-to-heart talk with someone. Confronting people can be frightening.

Most of us prefer to avoid confrontation. We have a wrong aversion to the very vehicle God has appointed to restore true peace between people. In Matt. 18:15 Jesus says, "If your brother sins against you, go and show him his fault, just between the two of you. If he listens to you, you have won your brother over." Don't shove feelings into a closet. Don't internalize frustration. Instead, be tough. Schedule a heart-to-heart talk and try to work out differences.

Prepare to Be Tough

Before making an appointment to get tough with somebody, it is important to prepare. First, *clarify the issue.* What exactly is causing the tension in the relationship? Is the problem temporary or lasting?

Second, *cleanse the spirit.* Jesus said in Matt. 7:3-5: "Why do you look at the speck of sawdust in your brother's eye and pay no attention to the plank in your own eye? How can you say to your brother, 'Let me take the speck out of your eye,' when all the time there is a plank in your own eye? You hypocrite, first take the plank out of your own eye, and then you will see clearly to remove the speck from your brother's eye."

In other words, if we feel critical, angry, and judgmental—if we can hardly wait to go in and wreak havoc—be careful. A heart-to-heart talk conducted with that attitude will not restore peace. Before calling our friend, we must surrender our spirit before God.

Third, *carefully select a time and place for the meeting.* For example, the wife of a football fanatic should not plan on meaningful dialogue during halftime of the Super Bowl. Likewise, a husband should not expect his wife to listen eagerly while she is fixing dinner, the baby is crying, and the two older children are fighting to the death in the next room. Plan to meet when both are physically fresh, when not hurried, and where privacy can be enjoyed.

Fourth, *pray.* God does amazing things when we ask Him.

Tough Does Not Mean Insensitive

Preparing properly for a confrontation wins half the battle. The other half is won when the heart-to-heart talk is conducted sensitively. Here are three steps that will help present the concerns clearly. They won't guarantee heartfelt thanks and "warm fuzzies" all around, but they will give the best possible chance of being listened to and respected.

First, *begin with a sincere statement of commitment to the relationship.* If talking to your spouse, tell him or her that the marriage is the most important relationship in the world and that it can get even better. If talking to a friend, tell him or her how much the friendship is appreciated. If in a work situation, tell the supervisor that work is enjoyable, or an employee that being on the team is pleasurable. In all cases let the person know that no ultimatum is being issued—we're just trying to work on a problem.

Second, *make a careful, nonaccusatory explanation of the issue.* Avoid saying, "You *always*" or "You *never.*" When one says, "You're never home, Frank," Frank will answer, "You're wrong. I was home two years ago on February 4. You have blown this all out of proportion." But if one says, "I feel alone so much, Frank. I feel neglected. I feel frustrated and confused," Frank is more likely to listen. He may think we're crazy for having certain feelings, but he can hardly deny that we're having them. State the problem as carefully as possible, using "I feel" statements whenever possible.

Third, *invite dialogue.* After spilling our heart on the matter, we ask, "Am I out to lunch on this? Do I have my facts straight? Am I missing something? Am I overly sensitive?"

The Results of Tough Love

Knowing the value of tough love, carefully prepared for a heart-to-heart confrontation, and having conducted it with wisdom and restraint, what possible outcomes can you expect?

I wish I could guarantee that the persons we love will say, "Thank you very much for bringing this to my attention." But it is not likely. We might get a slammed door, a pink slip, or an earful of angry words. We might end up in big trouble. But if our relationship is built on deception, we are in big trouble already. So take the risk, make some waves, and see what God does.

Most probably, the person will eventually take the words seriously, and your relationship will once again stand on firm ground. It is hard to resist someone who is humble and vulnerable. This may not happen immediately, however. Sometimes it takes several confrontations before the process is complete, and sometimes a relationship gets worse before it gets better. Some people excuse continuing hostilities by saying, "Well, I tried to patch it up once, and the other person wouldn't listen." But if a relationship has been disintegrating over months or years, reconciliation may take many attempts. It is unrealistic to expect one hour to undo the work of 10 years.

Unfortunately, despite our best efforts, sometimes the persons refuse to listen; and our relationship seems to be worse off than before. In that case, try mediation. Bring in someone both trust and respect, and let this person help with communication. A church may be able to help find a mediator—the pastor, perhaps, or members who have dedicated themselves to this task, or maybe a small-group leader. Or discuss the problems with a professional counselor. I especially recommend this when alcohol or drug abuse is involved. Mediation may bring good results we cannot obtain on our own.

But we might as well face the facts—in some cases, tough love brings on permanent division. Paul says, "If it is possible, *as far as it depends on you,* live at peace with everyone" (Rom. 12:18, emphasis added). But sometimes it isn't possible. For whatever reasons, sometimes two will separate and go different ways. Sometimes that is life in this sinful world. When it happens, we confess our sins, pick ourselves up, and by God's grace and with the help of our friends we go on.

Too many of us, however, give up without a fight when a relationship begins to disintegrate. We scrap and claw and even go to court to protect our property, but all we do is cry a little when relationships die. This is backward thinking. Relationships are worth fighting for. Love needs to be tough enough to hang on.

Jesus' love for us is the most tender love we will ever know. He died to heal our sins and to give us eternal life with Him. He guides, protects, comforts, and nourishes us with His Word. But Jesus' love is also the toughest love we will ever face. He knows our hearts and does not hesitate to tell us when He finds sin there. He insists on truth no matter how painful it may be. He loves us too much to allow us to continue unchecked down a path of self-destruction.

Real love is always both tender and tough. May God give us the sensitivity to know when to show each kind of love and the courage to do whatever love demands.

A cynic can chill and dishearten
with a single word.

RALPH WALDO EMERSON

Praise be to the God and Father of our Lord
Jesus Christ, the Father of compassion and the
God of all comfort, who comforts us in all our
troubles, so that we can comfort those in any
trouble with the comfort we ourselves
have received from God.

2 COR. 1:3-4

BACKGROUND SCRIPTURE
Jer. 31:29; Matt. 16:6; Rom. 12:2; Phil. 2:1-11

12

Accountable for an Attitude

by CARL M. LETH

IT WAS THE STRANGEST experience I have ever had while conducting a wedding ceremony. Our worship center is quite simple, so the wedding party had used some silk plants and two small, silk trees to form an attractive backdrop for the ceremony. The groom's family were not experienced churchgoers and were a little "rough around the edges." Nonetheless, everything was going well until we reached the ring ceremony. As I turned toward the best man to reach for the ring, something caught my attention. I glanced back. Barely three feet behind me, a video camera lens peeked through the scant branches of a silk tree. Operating the camera with a novice's enthusiasm was the groom's brother-in-law. Clearly visible to the entire congregation, he was a large man in a flannel shirt, sporting a bold baseball cap loudly proclaiming the brand name of a popular beer. In the course of the ceremony he had slipped in for a close-up. I regained my composure and finished the wedding. That cameraman's presence probably left a lasting impression on every person at that wedding. It did for me.

Our attitudes are like that amateur filmmaker. Perhaps in a less dramatic but no less certain way, our attitudes influence the experiences and impressions of those around us. John Wesley is

---

Dr. Carl Leth is senior pastor of the North Raleigh Church of the Nazarene in Raleigh, N.C.

often cited for his claim that there is no "solitary religion." Perhaps we could paraphrase him to say there is also no such thing as a "solitary attitude." That may not always be true, but it is usually true. Our attitudes, like our lives, intertwine with those around us. Yet, we usually talk about attitudes in a strictly personal way. In this chapter we would like to consider the issue of attitudes in community and relationships.

Take My Attitude and Pass It On

The truth is that attitudes are highly "catching." Our attitudes affect those around us, and their attitudes affect us. When I was in my last few weeks of duty as a marine, my sergeant told me I could have my last weeks off if I would stay away from the computer center where I worked. "You are already feeling and thinking like a civilian," he said, "and it is corrupting the other men." I think it was actually my growing happiness at my coming "liberation" that depressed the other marines, but whatever it was exerted a powerful influence on those in contact with me.

Attitudes have catching power. We are responsible for the stewardship of the influence of our attitudes. That raises the stakes on the importance of our attitudes. This includes a warning about the destructive influence of our negative attitudes on others. More constructively, it suggests the potential for positive influence of our good attitudes. The awareness of the power of attitudes in relationships cautions us to beware of the negative influence of others' attitudes on us. It also reminds us of our accountability for our influence on the attitudes of others. Our individual attitudes are a community issue.

A Little Goes a Long Way

Personal attitudes can exert surprising power. The impact they have on the attitude of a community is like that of yeast. Jesus recognized the multiplying impact of yeast, or leaven, and used it as an example. He referred to the powerful, negative effect of attitudes when He said, "Be on your guard against the yeast of the Pharisees and Sadducees" (Matt. 16:6). The power of attitudes can also work in a positive way. We all have a means of constructive service through the attitudes we show.

In our church we have only a few older people, but the ones we do have are very important. One lady named Frances plays an important role in our fellowship. She is a great-grandmother, a widow of modest means and declining health. Sometimes she has to endure significant pain to attend church services. Walking is difficult, and just getting to church is a major undertaking. However, her limited mobility doesn't keep her from carrying a bright smile and encouraging word with her wherever she goes. She leaves a wake of good feelings and positive attitudes behind her. I would say she has a ministry of attitude.

Marlene is another attitude minister. She is a younger woman, but her poor health denies her relief from constant pain. Her doctors can do little to help her. Most people in our church have no idea that she is constantly suffering. She encourages the people around her and helps them look at things from a positive perspective. She lifts them a little higher than when she found them. She leaves a contribution in the changed attitudes around her.

Both of these ladies reflect the power of positive influence in community like yeast as it permeates and expands dough. They lift the attitude of the community by their influence and example.

These positive examples should serve to suggest to us the reverse possibilities of negative attitudes. We probably can think of a negative example from our experience. We know people who can lower morale and change attitudes for the worse just by their presence. They can really make a difference in the attitudes of their community. A little poor attitude can go a long way!

Let Attitude Lead the Way

We need to say a word about the special role of leaders. Every person exerts influence through his or her attitudes. This is especially true for those in leadership roles. Pastors, for instance, can deeply influence the attitudes of their congregations. One of my more painful ministry experiences was as a member of our District Advisory Board. We were invited to meet with the pastor and church board of a troubled church. In the course of that meeting, local board members took turns telling us what they thought of us. It was ugly and mean-spirited. Throughout this ordeal the local pastor said very little. Perhaps he assumed that he could distance himself from this behavior by being silent. He wanted to show us that the laity held these attitudes on their own. The truth was that such negative attitudes could only have flourished in an environment where the pastor had tolerated, if not encouraged, them.

Leaders exert leadership in attitudes as well as other ways. Parents are leaders too. Find a family that is positive and upbeat in their attitudes. Then find the relational leader in that family. The dominant, or leading, personality will likely exhibit a positive attitude. The spirit that pervades an extended family is quickly recognized. The process is the same for families with negative, critical spirits. Each person is responsible for his or her own attitudes, but everyone begins with a model.

Jeremiah expresses this concept so graphically. "The fathers have eaten sour grapes, and the children's teeth are set on edge" (31:29). Even if our children say things we wouldn't say ourselves, we may be partially responsible. If their words give expression to attitudes they learned from us, then we have helped to author their "script."

Most of us exert leadership in some community. It may be in church, home, Sunday School class, or golf foursome. Anytime other people look to our example, we function as leaders. In all of those relationships we need to remember that our attitude helps to lead the way.

A Community Has an Attitude

Communities have attitudes. The attitudes of the members of the community are blended in a way that reflects the

outlook of the community as a whole. That viewpoint expresses the perspective and character of the community. It communicates the heart or spirit of that group of people.

When newcomers have contact with our communities,
they quickly sense our attitude. Visitors to our church "listen"
to the attitude of our congregation or Sunday School class.
Residents in our church's neighborhood probably have a distinct impression of our church's attitude. Our civic neighbors
in our town or city probably do too. Our attitude is a promi-
nent part of our witness. The public witness of our attitude
will either make our ministry more difficult or more effective.
One way or another, the attitude of our community will make
a difference in expressing a message about who we are.

Attitudes Are for Learning

The good news is that attitudes can be taught and
learned. A positive attitude is an acquired art, or skill, for most
of us. It is not a gift that we either have or don't have. We can
nurture and develop positive attitudes in our personal lives
and in our communities. Families can intentionally nurture
good attitudes and discourage the development of bad attitudes.

The same is true for churches. If our church fellowship
has developed some bad attitudes, we can work to change
them. If our church fellowship has developed good attitudes,
we need to be attentive to protect and encourage them. We
should consciously nurture our personal attitudes and those of
our communities. We should intentionally encourage the
learning of good attitudes.

A Beginning Place

Paul gives us some clear instruction about where to begin.
Phil. 2:1-11 is a Scripture lesson on attitude in community.
Paul's concern and desire for the Philippians is that they might
live in like-minded fellowship with a unity of purpose that is

mutually helpful. He envisions a community where members look for the betterment of the others in the group. Their actions would reflect that concern in the conduct of their lives. That sounds pretty good, doesn't it?

The key to realizing that kind of community is attitude. Specifically, it is the kind of attitude we can see in Jesus. In verses 6-11, Paul describes that attitude in one of the most beautiful and powerful passages in the Bible. If we could shape our attitudes by that vision, we would change our communities. We would be moved to thankfulness in the face of God's great love and sacrifice for us. Our perspective about our relationships with others would be molded by the memory of Jesus' attitude toward us. Our confidence for the future would be buoyed by the expectation of a great relationship with the exalted Christ.

In Rom. 12:2 Paul challenges us not to be conformed to this world, but to be transformed by the renewal of our minds. Jesus offers the model for that transformation. When our attitudes can be transformed into Christlikeness, our communities—including our churches and homes—will also be transformed.

Get an Attitude

So, get an attitude! Focus on Christ and get a good one. Help the community to get a good one too. Attitudes are not our enemies. They can be powerful allies. They can help make the difference. They can help us and our communities become what God wants for us to be at our best. Remember, like the cameraman at the wedding, each of us will have an impact on those around us. We are stewards of that influence. In our personal lives and in our communities we are accountable for an attitude. Let's make it count.

A man can fail many times, but he isn't a failure until he begins to blame somebody else.

JOHN BURROUGHS

Sitting down, Jesus called the Twelve and said, "If anyone wants to be first, he must be the very last, and the servant of all."

MARK 9:35

BACKGROUND SCRIPTURE
Phil. 2:1-13

13

An Attitude of Servanthood

by EARL LEE

THE HEART OF THE APOSTLE PAUL is never more open than when he writes a letter to the church at Philippi. He talks about being in chains, but really, he is very, very free.

Philippians 2:1-13 is a passage of scripture that we have dealt with theologically with great excitement. I wish we would move into it and live in it, coming face-to-face with the fact that it is also a very emotional passage of scripture.

We Have a Choice

For many years, I read the scripture, "Let this mind be in you, which was also in Christ Jesus" (Phil. 2:5, KJV). That was acceptable. But it was not penetrating, at least to me, until I came face-to-face with the fact that "mind" meant "attitude." The NIV puts it this way: "Your attitude should be the same as that of Christ Jesus." Then I knew what the apostle meant. It is an imitation. My attitude should be the *same* as that of Christ Jesus.

If we should say, "Everyone please *think* about doing this," that means an option exists. We *should* have this atti-

---

Dr. Earl Lee is the former pastor of the Pasadena (California) First Church of the Nazarene. He is now retired and lives with his wife, Hazel, in Wrightwood, California, where he enjoys being "happy and positive with a strong sense of humor."

tude. Anytime I see "should," it means I don't have to. "Should" is an invitation from the Holy Spirit through the apostle Paul to enter into the attitude of Jesus. There is a very basic realization here. The only thing I need to do is say "good morning" to this idea and face it. Nothing fits unless I, actually and personally, get down to what he is saying about my attitude. My attitude should be the same as that of Christ Jesus. Personally, I don't want to get out of that. I want to accept that invitation to get into what it means and then live there.

When our younger son, Grant, was getting his Ph.D. in psychology, he had his times of frustration. He would have breakfast with me. He would talk, and I would listen. In no way could I match his mind, but I listened to his frustrations. One morning what he was talking about had nothing to do with his studies. He said, "Dad, I am convinced that the deepest work of the Holy Spirit is in the area of attitudes."

The other day I was with our older son, Gary. He is the young man who was a hostage in Iran for 444 days. That was Easter, and on Tuesday, he was facing cancer surgery. His life was being jolted and turned around. While we were standing on a bridge on that beautiful afternoon, I told him what his brother had said about the Holy Spirit and attitudes. Without flashing an eye, which was something new for Gary, he said, "Dad, that is absolutely true, and I am finding that out now."

What Is an Attitude?

Attitude. I looked at the dictionary, which is always a book that can help us. An attitude is a mental position with regard to a fact or a state.

It was February 20, 1962, when a man by the name of John Glenn circled the earth in outer space three times; and we thought it was tremendous. We followed. We listened. We saw him on television. As I listened, I heard the words from a man in Houston who was guiding John Glenn. He said to him, "Your attitude must be changed a few degrees."

I thought, *That's a slip. He doesn't mean that. He means "altitude."* Later, a man who knows aeronautics said, "He meant exactly what he said. He meant that John Glenn's attitude must adjust itself to where he was—the position of an aircraft in relation to a given point of reference, usually on the ground level."

Not long ago I was given a tour through the Johnson Space Center in Houston. In Mission Control the guide pointed out five computers where specialists sit. Each of them is an authority in a different part of that mission, but they cannot talk to the astronauts in outer space. In front of these five is one person who gets all of the information from them. He is an astronaut himself, and he is the only one who talks to those in outer space. He speaks their language, and he knows how to communicate.

When I heard that, I thought, *Yes, there are many who have information, many who have ideas. But it is all channeled through the blessed Holy Spirit who speaks to me. He says, "This is the way, walk in it—to the left, to the right. This is what I want you to do—listen."* I can understand. Because He knows me, He is able to interpret to me exactly so that I might understand it. When He talks to me about altering my attitude, I don't debate it. He has said that to me many times during my life, and He keeps on saying it. I am used to saying now—sometimes with a struggle, but saying it—"Yes, Lord."

A Proper Attitude

It seems that a newly commissioned navy captain took great pride in his assignment as commander of a battleship. One stormy night, the captain saw a light moving steadily in their direction. He ordered the signalman to send the following message: "Change your course 10 degrees to the south."

The reply came back: "Change your course 10 degrees to the north."

The captain was determined not to give way to another

vessel, so he sent a countermessage: "Alter your direction 10 degrees. I am the captain."

The answer flashed back promptly: "Alter your direction; I am the lighthouse."

We laugh, but that is the same message we should hear. "I am the Lord; alter your attitude to Me." The altering of our attitude is to Christ Jesus. Not to a denomination. Not to a theological premise. Our attitude must be altered to Christ Jesus.

Jesus knew who He was. Today people say about anyone, "He doesn't know who he is." Or "He's just trying to find himself." Jesus knew who He was in the 13th chapter of John.

"It was just before the Passover Feast. Jesus knew that the time had come for him to leave this world and go to the Father. Having loved his own who were in the world, he now showed them the full extent of his love. . . . Jesus knew that the Father had put all things under his power and that he had come from God and was returning to God" (vv. 1, 3). It is hard to imagine what was in His hands. We're a world that's acquainted with power, but He had *all* power in His hands. He had every chance to take this whole world in His hands. Yet, "he got up from the meal, took off his outer clothing, and wrapped a towel around his waist. . . . he poured water into a basin and began to wash his disciples' feet, drying them with the towel that was wrapped around him" (vv. 4-5). The only thing that could be heard in that room was the dripping of water. "When he had finished washing their feet, he put on his clothes and returned to his place" (v. 12a).

He asked, "Do you understand what I have done for you?" (v. 12b). Of course, they thought they did. "You call me 'Teacher' and 'Lord,' and rightly so . . . Now that I, your Lord and Teacher, have washed your feet, you also should wash one another's feet. I have set you an example that you should do as I have done for you. I tell you the truth, no servant is greater than his master" (vv. 13-16).

So, I'm face-to-face with the attitude that was in Christ Jesus. I must totally relinquish myself to what He is saying. He made himself nothing. He took the very nature of a servant, the true attitude of a servant. He emptied himself of all that He had. And He said this is what I should do. How opposite to our way of thinking today! We ask, "What can I get out of it?"

The Highest Attitude

The Master that we follow said the highest position we can reach is a servant. Our greatest mission to our world today is servanthood. We have to choose to be a servant. Not everyone wants to be a servant.

Having lived in India, I know servants are a part of life there. But many want to be a servant only until they can get somebody else to be their servant. Very few choose servanthood as a way of life, because a servant has to give himself or herself totally to the master. One has to know the master. One must listen, which is equal to obeying totally the master's desire, and that is rare. And yet Jesus boldly confronts us: "Why not have this attitude—the attitude of Jesus Christ, the attitude of servanthood?"

When we went to India in 1946, we had to study the language. We had to have someone watch our little daughter, Gayle. A lady came into our life, a field woman who knew no English. She was a Hindu and had never been inside a home where white people lived. She was recommended and came to our house.

Muktabi was an idol worshiper. One day she came into the room where Hazel, my wife, was praying. Walking in bare feet, Muktabi did not make any noise. After she had finished her prayer time, Hazel got up and wiped tears from her eyes. Muktabi watched her. A few days later, Hazel came back into the same room; and Muktabi was there, sitting beside the carriage of our little girl. She was crying. Hazel asked what she was crying about. She replied, "The other day I watched you praying. I looked around and saw no idol. But I saw your face, and it was a beautiful face, with tears. Today, I thought, *I want to talk to God, and there are no idols; but I will talk to Him to the best of my ability.* And I found Jesus as my Savior."

Muktabi stayed in our life for many years, as long as we were in India. During our first term, we had diphtheria. Hazel had diphtheria; she was in one bed. Gary had diphtheria; he was in another bed in the same room. Even baby Gayle had diphtheria and was in the crib.

I had to do everything. I was the orderly, the doctor, the chaplain—everything. I ran from one to the other. Because I had diphtheria as a young fellow, I was immune. The most troubling part was that Gayle needed constant attention. Muktabi came to me and said, "I'll come in and take care of Gayle."

I said, "You can't do that. You'll take diphtheria."

She said, "Oh, that doesn't make any difference."

But I said, "Muktabi, you'll have to stay 24 hours a day. You can't come in and go out."

"Oh," she said, "that doesn't make any difference. I want to sit by the side of my Gayle."

But I insisted, "Muktabi, you don't understand. This is a disease that can kill you."

"Oh," she said, "that has nothing to do with it. I will come in."

I reminded her, "That will mean that you'll have to have food through the window. We'll try to cleanse the dish and send it out, and I have no idea how long it will be."

"That makes no difference," she responded with a smile. She came in and sat by Gayle's little crib night and day. Anytime Gayle would stir, Muktabi would be there. She completely took all of the worry for Gayle off my heart and Hazel's heart as well. The siege lasted night and day. At the end of two weeks, the diphtheria was finished. We were given clearance and to go out and face our world. Muktabi, too, had clearance.

Most say, "Tell me how God spared her." I can't. She caught diphtheria and became very ill. With it she took a special and very difficult heart ailment. But in all of 14 years in India, I never heard Muktabi say one negative word about that experience. She loved our little girl and she loved us. She served every interest of our lives. No questions asked. No conditions. No small type. She was a servant!

A Healthy Response

I have to linger over this passage in Philippians. I have to live in it. I have to come to grips with what it means to be a servant. I cannot wait until I can be elevated. Jesus' life on earth demonstrated that He was never elevated from being a servant. If I follow Him, I will never be elevated from being a servant. He made himself nothing.

A. C. Chakravati became a good friend of mine in India. One time he said, "Do you know what 'Jesus is Lord' means?" I thought I knew, but the way he asked, I knew he wanted to tell me. So he said, "Jesus is Lord means He is my Owner, He is my Possessor, He is my Repossessor."

I never forgot that. If Jesus is Lord, that means He owns me. *He owns me!* Nothing withheld from Him. I am merely the steward over anything I have. There is nothing that I have that I own. He is the Owner. He is my Owner if I am learning to be a servant. He possesses me. He lives in this body. His attitude is my desire. He lives in my mind. I can trust my thoughts. When they are not according to what He wants, He lets me know.

He not only owns me and possesses me but also may repossess anything I have at any time. If I am a servant, and if my Master says, "The keys, please," there may be a bit of a struggle. We're human. Finally, I reach in and say, "Lord, here are the keys. My business. My church. My body. The keys are yours." Because He is Lord, my "attitude should be the same as that of Christ Jesus" (Phil. 2:5).

I have to face such possibilities by saying my attitude *will* be the same as that of Christ Jesus—which is to be a servant, at which I have been working now for many years. I want to learn from Jesus what it means to be a servant. The only way I learn to be a servant is to live with Jesus. As I live with Him, He corrects my attitude, brings it into line. I can say, "Thank You for what You are teaching me." It's an attitude. I'm in charge of my attitudes. I can choose.